READING AND WRITING Sourcebook

Authors

Ruth Nathan
Laura Robb

Great Source Education Group

a Houghton Mifflin Company

Authors

Ruth Nathan one of the authors of *Writers Express* and *Write Away*, is the author of many professional books and articles on literacy. She earned a Ph.D. in reading from Oakland University in Rochester, Michigan, where she co-headed their reading research laboratory for several years. She currently teaches in third grade, as well as consults with numerous schools and organizations on reading.

Laura Robb author of *Reading Strategies That Work* and *Teaching Reading in the Middle School*, has taught language arts at Powhatan School in Boyce, Virginia, for more than thirty years. She also mentors and coaches teachers in Virginia public schools and speaks at conferences throughout the country.

Contributing Writer

Anina Robb is a writer and a teacher. She earned an M.F.A. in Poetry from Sarah Lawrence College and an M.A. in English from Hollins College. Ms. Robb taught English for four years in public schools in New York City.

Table of Contents

Be an Active Reader

When you read, do you mark up the text? Do you write down questions about your reading? Active readers read with a pen in hand. They make notes, underline, and draw. It's easy to become an active reader.

Read the 4 poems on the next pages and see the examples of how one active reader took notes. You too can **draw, question, make clear,** and **connect** to the reading.

I. DRAW

You can **draw** to help you "see" what you read. Here the reader has drawn a little tree. The picture shows what the poet says in the poem.

Response Notes

"Little Pine" by Wang Jian

My little pine tree is just a few
   feet tall.
It doesn't even have a trunk yet.
I keep measuring myself against it
But the more I watch it, the slower
   it grows.

QUESTION

You can mark a text to make important parts stand out and then ask **questions**. Mark the readings in this book by circling, underlining, or highlighting. Here a reader has underlined "white feathers" and "red feet" and asks, "Do all geese look like this?"

"Goose" by Luo Bin-Wang

Goose! Goose! Goose!
Turn your neck and sing at
    the sky,
Glide your <u>white feathers</u> over
    the green water,
Paddle your <u>red feet</u> in the clear
    waves.

Response Notes

Do all geese
have white
feathers and
red feet?

MAKE CLEAR

You can **make clear** what you read by writing notes. That way you know what is happening in the reading. Here the notes remind the reader. They make it clear that, after a spring storm, trees lose some of their blossoms.

Response Notes

Blossoms fall
after a storm.

"Spring Sleep"
by Meng Hao-Ran

Sleepily waking to a spring dawn
I hear birds singing everywhere.
After last night's wind and rain
How many <u>blossoms</u> have fallen?

blossoms (blos•soms)—flowers.

IV.

CONNECT

As you read, think about what the reading means to you. How do you feel about it? How can you **connect** it to your own life? How is it like something you know? How has the reader connected his or her feeling to the poem?

"Moon" by Li Bai

When I was little
I thought the moon was a white
  <u>jade</u> plate,
Or maybe a mirror in Heaven
Flying through the blue clouds.

jade—precious stone.

Response Notes

I used to think there was a man on the moon!

How to Read a Lesson

Here are 3 easy steps to help you get the most out of the readings in this book.

1. For each reading, **read it once** and just circle or underline the important parts.

2. Then **read it again.** On the second reading, write questions or comments in the Notes.

3. Then, at the end of each reading, you will find a part called **Reread.** This part asks you to go back one more time and be sure you have answered all the questions.

Red=Follow Directions

Blue=Write Here

Black=Read This

READ
Read this part of the biography of Booker T. Washington.
1. On the first reading, underline parts of the story that make you wonder what Booker's life was like.
   On the next reading, write in the Notes the **questions** that popped into your head.

Booker T. Washington
by Patricia and Fredrick McKissack

Booker Taliaferro Washington never knew his birthday. He was born a slave, and the dates of slave births were not always written down. It is believed he was born sometime in 1856.

Booker and his family lived on a large Virginia plantation. Their one-room shack had a dirt floor. The door didn't shut well. The windows had no glass. There were cracks in the walls.

Booker didn't even have a bed. He slept on the floor next to his brother John and his sister Amanda. A fireplace warmed the cabin. But it was always too hot or too cold in their home.

plantation (plan•ta•tion)—large farm where slaves would often live and work.
shack—small, poorly-built cabin.

Response Notes

EXAMPLE:
How many people lived there?

© GREAT SOURCE. COPYING IS PROHIBITED.

13

reread

Read *Booker T. Washington* one more time. As you do, look for answers to the questions you wrote in the Notes. Be sure you have answered all of the **Stop and Think** questions.

By reading and rereading, you will do what good readers do.

Booker T. Washington

What do you think of when you hear the word *freedom*? How would your life be different if you could not go to school, ride in a bus, or get paid for doing a job? Booker T. Washington was not a free person, but his life was soon to change.

BEFORE YOU READ

Have you ever tried to figure out what will happen next? When you do this, you are using clues in the story and what you know to make a prediction.

1. Read the 4 sentences from *Booker T. Washington*.
2. Tell what you think the reading will be about.

• "Booker and his family lived on a large Virginia plantation."
• "A fireplace warmed the cabin."
• "One day Booker passed by a school."
• "In 1863, President Abraham Lincoln freed all slaves in the South."

My prediction:

....
....
....
....
....
....

MY PURPOSE

Who was Booker T. Washington, and what was his life like?

I. READ

Read this part of the biography of Booker T. Washington.
1. On the first reading, underline parts of the story that make you wonder what Booker's life was like.
2. On the next reading, write in the Notes the **questions** that popped into your head.

Booker T. Washington
by Patricia and Fredrick McKissack

Booker Taliaferro Washington never knew his birthday. He was born a slave, and the dates of slave births were not always written down. It is believed he was born sometime in 1856.

Booker and his family lived on a large Virginia plantation. Their one-room shack had a dirt floor. The door didn't shut well. The windows had no glass. There were cracks in the walls.

Booker didn't even have a bed. He slept on the floor next to his brother John and his sister Amanda. A fireplace warmed the cabin. But it was always too hot or too cold in their home.

plantation (plan•ta•tion)—large farm where slaves would often live and work.
shack—small, poorly built cabin.

Response Notes

EXAMPLE:

How many people lived there?

13

What was Booker T. Washington's home like?

Response Notes

BOOKER T. WASHINGTON (continued)

When Booker was five years old, his master put him to work. Booker fanned flies away from his master's table at mealtimes.

When he got older, he was given a new job. Every week he went to the mill with a load of corn. The corn was <u>ground</u> into <u>meal</u> there.

STOP AND THINK **stop and think** STOP AND THINK

What 2 jobs did Booker T. Washington have?

ground—crushed into powder.
meal—ground corn that people eat.

Response Notes

One day Booker passed by a school. He wanted to go inside. But slave children could not go to school. It was against the law!

In 1861 the Civil War began. Northern and Southern states were at war with each other.

Lots of people wanted to end slavery. In 1863, President Abraham Lincoln freed all slaves in the South. But some slaves didn't know they were free until the war ended in 1865.

Northern soldiers came to the plantation where Booker and his family lived. The soldiers said they were free. There was a lot of singing and shouting. Freedom had come at last!

← reread →

Read *Booker T. Washington* one more time. As you do, look for answers to the questions you wrote in the Notes. Be sure you have answered all of the **Stop and Think** questions.

WORD WORK

You can make a long word by joining 2 small words. The long word is called a **compound word**. Look at these examples:

out + side = *outside*   friend + ship = *friendship*

1. Skim *Booker T. Washington*. Find 4 compound words.
2. Write the compound words and small words below in the chart. One example has been done for you.

Compound Word	Small Word	Small Word
sometime	some	time
1.		
2.		
3.		
4.		

READING REMINDER

Predicting before you read and asking questions while you read can help you understand the story better.

III. GET READY TO WRITE

A. BRAINSTORM

The story ends with Booker and his family discovering they are free. Their lives are about to change. Pretend you are Booker T. Washington and you are writing a letter to a friend.

1. Brainstorm a list of the things that you might do now that you are free.
2. Write your list in the box below. The first one has been done for you.

Things that I might do now that I am free:

1. Our family might move to a new house.

2.

3.

4.

17

B. STUDY A MODEL

Here are the 5 parts of a friendly letter.

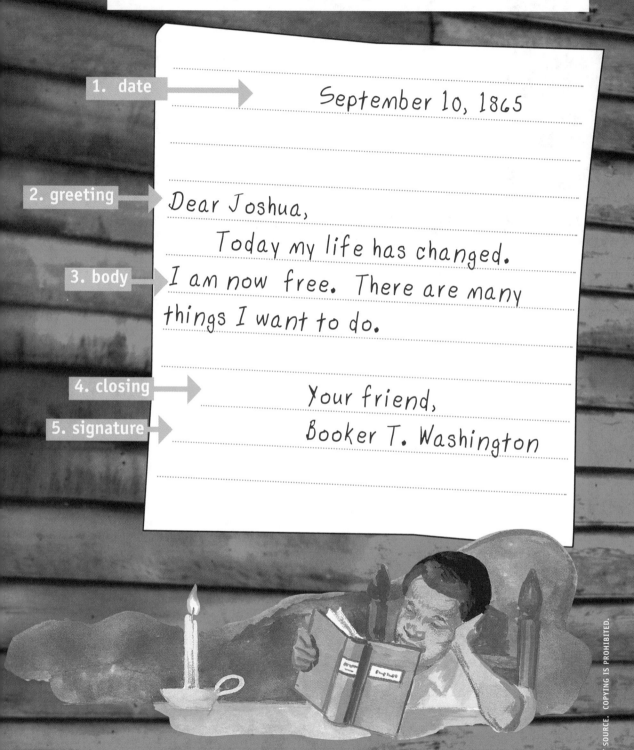

1. date

September 10, 1865

2. greeting

Dear Joshua,

3. body

Today my life has changed.
I am now free. There are many
things I want to do.

4. closing

Your friend,

5. signature

Booker T. Washington

 ## WRITE

Now you are ready to write your own **letter**. Pretend to be Booker T. Washington and tell your friend the things you might do now that you are free.

1. Check the 3 ideas from your brainstorming list that you want to include.

2. Review the friendly letter model on page 18.

3. Use the Writers' Checklist to edit your letter.

Continue writing on the next page.

Continue your letter.

_____

_____

_____

_____

_____

_____

V. LOOK BACK

What part of Booker T. Washington's life did you enjoy reading about? Why? Write your answer below.

_____

_____

Gloria's Way

What is the most important thing for a friend to do? Keep a secret? Stand up for you? Listen to your feelings? Sometimes it is not easy to share a friend. Find out the trouble Gloria has with her friend.

BEFORE YOU READ

Read the statements below about friendship.

1. If you agree, check the AGREE box. If you disagree check the DISAGREE box.
2. Share ideas with your reading partner.

AGREE	DISAGREE	
☐	☐	Good friends should be just like you.
☐	☐	Your best friend should be your only true friend.
☐	☐	Sometimes friends do not say what they feel.
☐	☐	Friendships always come to an end.
☐	☐	Friends can sometimes have trouble with each other.

What do you think <u>Gloria's Way</u> will be about?

....

....

....

....

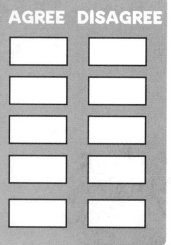

MY PURPOSE

What trouble is Gloria having with her friend?

READ

Read this part of the novel *Gloria's Way*.

1. On the first reading, circle parts of *Gloria's Way* that make you think about friendship.
2. On the second reading, **connect** what happens to your feelings and experiences. Write your thoughts in the Notes.

Gloria's Way by Ann Cameron

Response Notes

My mom sat down on the edge of my bed. "Gloria," she said, "would you really want Julian to like you best just because you were the only friend he had? That's what you're saying, really."

"It was nicer before," I said.

"Gloria," my mom said, "wanting one person all to yourself isn't wanting a friend. It's wanting a <u>prisoner</u>!"

"I don't want Julian to be my prisoner," I told her. "I just want him to like me best."

prisoner (pris•on•er)—someone who is kept away from most people and who is not free.

EXAMPLE:
I know the feeling— just like what happened in 2nd grade.

23

"If you want him to like you best, you'll have to let him be free," my mom said.

"He *is* free," I said. "I just want to know who he likes better. When I'm well, I'm going to ask him!"

DOUBLE-ENTRY JOURNAL

Quote	What You Think It Means
" 'If you want him to like you best, you'll have to let him be free,' my mom said."	

GLORIA'S WAY (continued)

"Ask him if you want," my mom said. "But remember, it may not work."

"It will!" I said. "Julian always tells me everything!"

"Don't be too sure," my mom said. "Sometimes people don't want to say what they feel. Sometimes they don't tell the truth. There is an old saying, Gloria: 'Actions speak louder than words.' Watch Julian's actions, and you can guess how he feels."

"But I don't want to guess!" I said. "I want to *know!*"

My mom <u>sighed</u>. "You'll have to do things your own way, I suppose. Just don't expect it to work out the way you want."

I frowned and pulled my covers up to my neck.

sighed—made a noise and breathed out deeply, often done when someone is tired.

My mom smoothed my covers. She smoothed my forehead.

"Gloria," she said, "there isn't a <u>measuring stick</u> you can put to friendship. When you start measuring too much, it's like digging up a plant in the garden to see how it's growing. If you dig it up too many times, it will die."

"Friendships die?" I said.

JOURNAL

DOUBLE-ENTRY

Quote	What You Think It Means
" ' Gloria,' she said, 'there isn't a measuring stick you can put to friendship.' "	

"Sometimes," my mom said. "But then new ones grow."

"I want the ones I have now!" I said.

"Listen, Gloria," my mom said.

measuring stick (meas•ur•ing stick)—stick marked with distances, which can be used to tell exactly how long a certain object is.

GLORIA'S WAY (continued)

"This is a hard truth, but I am going to tell it to you anyway. Friends come and go, but your best friend is always you. As long as *you* like you, lots of other people will, and deep down you'll be happy."

I sat up. My bed jiggled my bedside table, and the table jiggled my soup. My mom moved the table away from the bed.

"How can I be my best friend?" I said. "I'm only just one person!"

"You need to learn to talk to yourself," my mom said. "For instance, you might say to yourself, 'I know you're tired of being sick, and it's not your fault that you're sick, and you're very

good and <u>patient</u> not to complain.' Like that," my mom explained.

My mom went back to her work, and I ate my soup. Afterward, I tried being my best friend. I thanked myself for eating all my soup, and I told myself that I was a nice person even if I was sick, and that I liked me very, very much.

I thought some more about Julian, and then I fell asleep.

patient (pa•tient)—being calm even if you are going through pain or difficulty.

reread

Reread *Gloria's Way*. As you do, think about what friendship means to you. Be sure you have responded to each quote in the **Double-entry Journals.**

WORD WORK

Many words you know end in a final *silent e*: *taste*, *smile*, *make*. Words that end in a final *silent e* are tricky to read when a suffix is added that begins with a vowel, such as *-ed*, *-ing*, and *-er*. They are tricky to read because the *silent e* is dropped, so the base word looks strange: *make–making*. Remember this simple rule:

If a word ends in a *silent e*, drop the *e* before adding a suffix that starts with a vowel.

1. Add suffixes to each word in the chart below.
2. One has been done for you.

Word	+ed	+ing
rake	raked	raking
1. edge		
2. like		
3. measure		
4. suppose		

READING REMINDER

Making connections between your own ideas and experiences and what characters think and do helps you understand and enjoy a story.

GET READY TO WRITE

ORGANIZE YOUR IDEAS

Get ready to write a journal entry on what friendship means to you. Brainstorm a list of ideas about friendship.

1. Use the web below to organize your ideas.
2. Study the examples and add to them.

What does a good friend do?

1. Talks to me when I am sad

2.

How do you make friends?

1.

2.

friendship

What does a good friend say?

1. "I know what you mean!"

2.

What makes a best friend?

1.

2.

IV.  WRITE

Write a **journal entry** about what friendship means to you.

1. Use ideas from your web on page 30.
2. Finish with a closing sentence that says how a good friend makes you feel.
3. Use the Writers' Checklist to help you edit your journal entry.

Friendship means many things to me.

Continue writing on the next page.

Continue your journal entry.

V. LOOK BACK

Which parts of *Gloria's Way* were easy to read and which parts were hard? Why? Write your answers below.

Train to Somewhere

Long ago in America many orphans rode west on Orphan Trains. They were looking for families who would adopt them. How would you feel riding to a strange place in search of a new family?

I. BEFORE YOU READ

Get ready to read *Train to Somewhere* by thinking about the sentences below.

1. If you agree with a sentence, put a ✔.

2. If you disagree with a sentence, put an X.

3. Share your answers with your reading partner.

✔ agree X disagree

_____ A. Every child needs a good home.

_____ B. Children who don't have parents should live with new families.

_____ C. Brothers and sisters should live together.

_____ D. Adults do not like messy children.

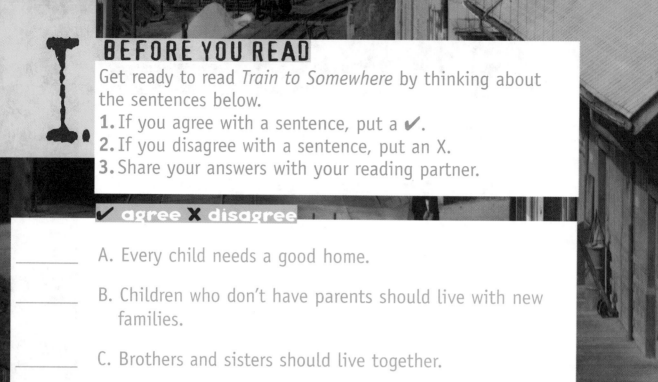

MY PURPOSE
What was it like to ride on an Orphan Train?

II. READ

Read the following part of *Train to Somewhere*.
1. On your first reading, underline details that show what riding the Orphan Train was like.
2. On your next reading, write statements in the Notes that **make clear** what you're learning about orphans who rode west on orphan trains.

Train to Somewhere
by Eve Bunting

"This is our train, Marianne," Miss Randolph says, and Nora <u>clutches</u> at my hand.

A <u>conductor</u> comes along the <u>platform</u>. "Are these the orphans, ma'am?" he asks.

Miss Randolph stands very straight. "<u>Fourteen of them</u>."

"We put on a special <u>coach</u> for you at the back," the conductor says.

The big boys carry the trunks and we take the rest of the <u>bundles</u>. Miss

clutches (clutch•es)—grabs and holds tightly.
conductor (con•duct•or)—person who drives and is in charge of the train.
platform (plat•form)—place where someone waits for a train.
coach—railroad car.
bundles (bun•dles)—packages.

Response Notes

EXAMPLE:
Orphans would travel in groups.

Randolph brings the <u>emergency bag</u>. This past week I watched her pack it with washcloths, medicine, and <u>larkspur</u> in case there are some <u>stowaway fleas</u>. None of us from St. Christopher's has any, of course. But those from the other homes and from the streets might.

emergency bag (e•mer•gen•cy bag)—bag with supplies for sudden, new problems.
larkspur (lark•spur)—kind of flower with a strong smell.
stowaway fleas (stow•a•way fleas)—small, hard-to-see insects that attach themselves to people or animals.

TRAIN TO SOMEWHERE (continued)

Response Notes

"Going for a placing-out, are you?" the conductor asks Nora. "My, you look nice!"

"Thank you," Nora says. She's only five, but at St. Christopher's they teach us manners early.

"Good luck!" he says to me. "I hear there are still a lot of people in the New West wanting children to adopt."

"Yes, indeed," Miss Randolph says.

"We're not seeing as many going this year as last, though," the conductor adds. "1877 was a peak year for orphans."

We go aboard.

The train seats are hard.

peak year—year in which the most orphans rode the Orphan Trains.
aboard (a•board)—into the train.

STOP AND THINK stop and think STOP AND THINK

Why are the orphans going to the New West?

I let Nora sit by the window. We can see ourselves <u>reflected</u> in its dirty glass. She's wearing her new blue coat with the shiny buttons.

Her hair twirls in bright <u>ringlets</u> under her <u>bonnet</u>. I can see my own long, thin face. I'm not pretty. I know Nora will be one of the first ones taken.

"Marianne?" She's got my hand again. "Will they believe we're sisters? We don't look a bit alike. I couldn't bear it if they split us up.

Let's not go if . . ."

"Shh!" I whisper.

But Miss Randolph has heard. "What's this?" she asks. "It won't work pretending to be sisters." Her voice softens. "Girls, listen. Most of the

reflected (re•flect•ed)—formed an image of something, as in a mirror.
ringlets (ring•lets)—long curls.
bonnet (bon•net)—cloth hat held in place by a string that ties under the chin.

TRAIN TO SOMEWHERE (continued)

people will only want one child. Don't <u>spoil</u> it for each other."

It's all right, I tell myself. I slide my fingers into my pocket and touch the softness of the feather. *She'll be there. She'll want me.*

stop and **think**

Why is Marianne worried?

The train's moving. We're gliding fast and smooth past <u>freight yards</u>, past <u>tenements</u> with washing <u>strung</u> on lines, past <u>warehouses</u>. Then we're in the country and there are trees, trees with apples hanging on them.

spoil—ruin.
freight yards—place where trains pick up and drop off their cars containing goods.
tenements (ten•e•ments)—rundown apartments.
strung—hung on strings.
warehouses (ware•hous•es)—places where goods are stored.

I knew this was the way apples grew but I'd never seen such a thing before.

Miss Randolph has me and another big girl, Jean, hold up a blanket to separate the boys from the girls. She opens one of the trunks and gives us our old clothes. We're to change.

"We don't want you looking messy at the first stop," she says.

She holds the blanket for Jean and me. We fold our new clothes and put them back into the trunks.

After a while we make sandwiches from the loaves and

Response Notes

fillings Miss Randolph has brought and we have thick milk out of a can. When it gets dark we sleep, sitting up, leaning against one another.

The wheels <u>mumble</u> all night long.

> *Clickety-clack, clickety-clee,*
> *I'm coming, Mama. Wait*
> *for me.*

At Chicago we carry everything out and change trains. Then we're on our way again.

mumble (mum•ble)—make noises that are not clear.

reread

Reread *Train to Somewhere*. Think about the details you underlined and be sure you have answered all the **Stop and Think** questions.

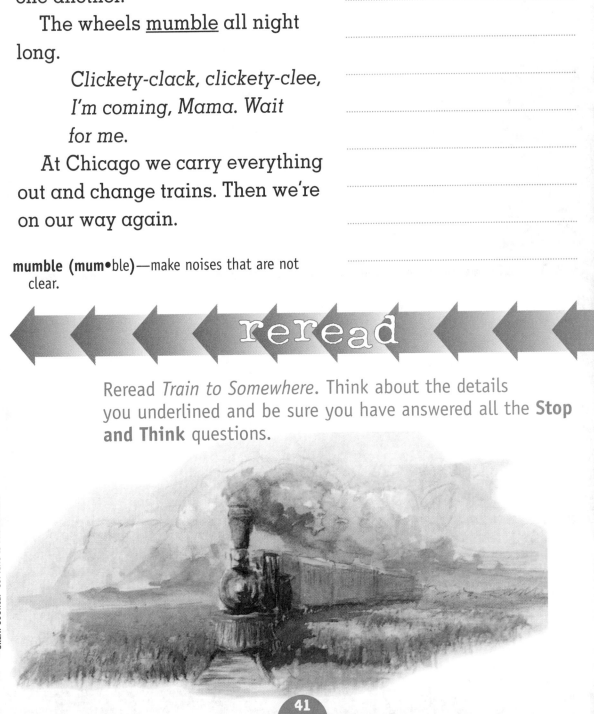

WORD WORK

Many words you read sound the same, but they have a different spelling. We call these words **homophones.** Here are some homophones from *Train to Somewhere.*

two, to   one, won   see, sea

1. Read the homophones and examples below.

   they're—a contraction for *they are*—
   Example: *They're on time today.*

   their—shows ownership—
   Example: *The red one is their car.*

   there—points out direction—
   Example: *There is the barn.*

2. Now write the correct homophone (**they're, their, there**) in the blank in each sentence below.

1. The ball rolled down the hill and landed over_____.

2. We camped at _____summer cabin.

3. _____meeting us at the movie theater.

4. The Smiths' new car is in _____garage.

5. _____are the goats and sheep.

6. After the party,_____going home.

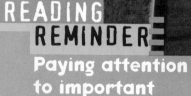

READING REMINDER

Paying attention to important details helps you better understand what you read.

III. GET READY TO WRITE

A. PLAN A PARAGRAPH

Get ready to write a paragraph about what life was like for an orphan riding the Orphan Train. Your paragraph needs a beginning, a middle, and an end.

1. Work on the beginning. The first sentence is called a topic sentence. It tells what the paragraph will be about.
2. Use the formula below to write your topic sentence.

A SPECIFIC TOPIC

+ A FEELING ABOUT THE TOPIC

= A GOOD TOPIC SENTENCE

Example: Orphans heading west had to experience a lot
(topic)
of new and frightening things.
(feeling)

My closing sentence:

_____
(topic)

_____
(feeling)

B. BUILD A PARAGRAPH

Work on the **middle** of your paragraph.
1. List 4 kinds of details that will help support your topic sentence.
2. Then describe each event in the box underneath. One has been done for you.

DETAIL 1
What they wear

DETAIL 2

DETAIL 3

DETAIL 4

The orphans have new clothes for when the train stops.

C. WRITE A CLOSING

Work on the **end.** The last sentence is called the closing, or wrap-up, sentence. It restates the topic of your paragraph.
1. Study the example.
2. Then write your own closing on the line below.

Example: *Getting used to new things was just part of life for orphans riding on Orphan Trains.*

My closing sentence:

IV. WRITE

Now, you are ready to write your own **expository paragraph** about what riding the Orphan Trains was like.

1. Begin with your topic sentence.
2. Pick 3 details from page 44 to support your topic sentence.
3. Finish your paragraph with your closing sentence.
4. Use the Writers' Checklist to edit your paragraph.

Title:

Continue writing on the next page.

Continue your paragraph.

....

....

....

....

....

....

....

V. LOOK BACK

What did you learn from *Train to Somewhere?* Write your answer below.

....

....

....

....

....

....

....

First Flight

Imagine you could fly like a bird. What would it feel like? What would the world look like? Would your friends believe you? What things could you do if you could fly?

BEFORE YOU READ

One word or idea can be very important to a story. Making a web can help you better understand what the word or idea means.

1. With a partner, discuss the term *flying machine*. What does it mean to you? What does it mean to your partner?
2. On the web below, list words, phrases, or places that you think of when you hear the words *flying machine*.

Flying Machine

MY PURPOSE

What are flying machines? Who invented them?

READ

Read this part of the book *First Flight*.

1. Pay attention to details that tell you about flying machines.
2. In the Notes, **draw** pictures of what you "see" in your mind as you read.

First Flight by George Shea

Kitty Hawk, North Carolina

One morning, Tom Tate went out fishing. The first fish he caught was too little, so he threw it back. Then he caught a bigger fish.

"This could feed me and Pa for days," he said to himself.

Down the beach, Tom saw two men near a big tent. Tom walked over to see what they were doing.

"Hello," said one of the men. "That's a big fish you've got there."

"You should have seen the first one I caught!" said Tom. "It was as big as a whale. It was so big, I couldn't even pull it up on the beach."

The men laughed. They wore funny clothes. Tom could see they weren't from Kitty Hawk.

Response Notes

EXAMPLE:

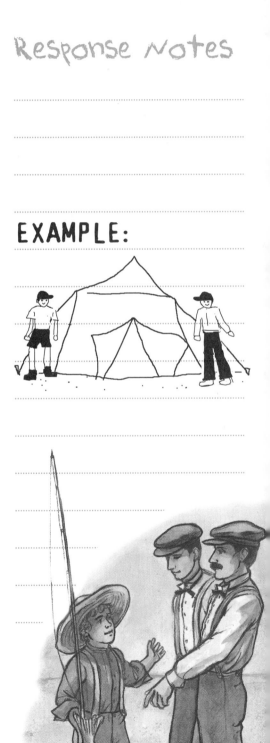

Quote	What You Think It Means
"They wore funny clothes. Tom could see they weren't from Kitty Hawk."	

Response Notes

FIRST FLIGHT (continued)

"My name is Orville. Orville Wright," said one of the men. "You can call me Orv. This is my brother, Wilbur."

"Call me Will," said the other man.

"I'm Tom Tate," said Tom. "What are you doing here in Kitty Hawk?"

"We came here from Ohio to build a flying machine," said Will.

"What's that?" asked Tom.

"See for yourself," said Will. "This machine will fly through the air."

"What makes it fly?" Tom asked.

"The same thing that makes a kite fly—the wind," said Orv. "That's why we came to Kitty

FIRST FLIGHT (continued)

Hawk. This is one of the windiest places in America."

"The sand makes a soft place to land, too," added Will.

"Can I ride on it?" asked Tom.

"It's not finished yet," said Will, "but come back later and we will see."

"Okay," said Tom. "I will."

DOUBLE-ENTRY JOURNAL

Quote	What You Think It Means
"'What makes it fly?' Tom asked. 'The same thing that makes a kite fly—the wind,' said Orv."	

Tom was <u>imagining</u> himself flying through the air when he ran into his cousins Ned and Laura.

"I just met two men from Ohio," Tom said. "They say they are going to fly through the air like birds!"

"Oh, Tom," said Laura, "don't tell us more of your silly stories."

"It's true," said Tom. "They showed me a flying machine they've built."

"There aren't any such things as flying machines," said Ned. "You're making it up."

"Just wait," said Tom. "You'll see."

imagining (i•**mag**•in•ing)—pretending; thinking about doing something you are not really doing.

reread

Reread *First Flight*. This time be sure you have responded to each quote in the **Double-entry Journals**.

WORD WORK

You can take 2 words and make them into 1 new word.

can not = *can't*   he will = *he'll*   could not = *couldn't*

We call these new words **contractions**. When you read a contraction, think of the two small words that make it up.

1. Look at each pair of words in the chart below.
2. Then write the contraction form.
3. Make sure you use an apostrophe (') to take the place of the missing letter(s). One example has been done for you.

Two Words	Contraction
were not	weren't
1. I am	
2. it is	
3. you have	
4. you will	
5. do not	
6. that is	
7. they have	

READING REMINDER

Making pictures in your head or seeing the people, places, and action in a story helps you remember the story.

II. GET READY TO WRITE

GATHER INFORMATION

Pretend you are a news reporter. You have to write a news story about 2 men trying out a flying machine in Kitty Hawk, North Carolina.

1. News stories have a headline and answer 5 questions: Who? What? When? Where? and Why? These are called the **5 Ws**.
2. Use the chart to list your **5 Ws**.
3. Add a closing sentence that tells how the world will change when people can fly.

Headline: *Brothers Try Flying in a Machine*

Who:

What:

When: 1902

Where:

Why:

Closing Sentence:

IV. WRITE

Now you are ready to write a **news story**.

1. First write a headline.
2. Then tell the who, what, when, where, and why of your news story.
3. Write a closing sentence about how this flying machine may change the future.
4. Use the Writers' Checklist to edit your news story.

Headline: _____

Continue writing on the next page.

Continue your news story.

....

....

....

....

....

....

....

....

LOOK BACK

How would you tell someone what *First Flight* was about?
Write your answer below.

....

....

....

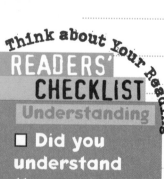

....

....

A Drop of Blood

Do you ever wonder how the air you breathe gets
into your body? Do you know how the food you
eat helps you grow? Read on to find out
how blood helps you live.

I. BEFORE YOU READ

Previewing lets you think about parts of a text before you read it. It starts you thinking about the topic.

1. Read the first and last paragraphs of *A Drop of Blood*.
2. Look at the art and pictures. What do they suggest the reading will be about?
3. Read the underlined words. Read the sentence that includes each underlined word.
4. In your own words, answer each question.

• What is this reading about?

• What questions do you have about this topic?

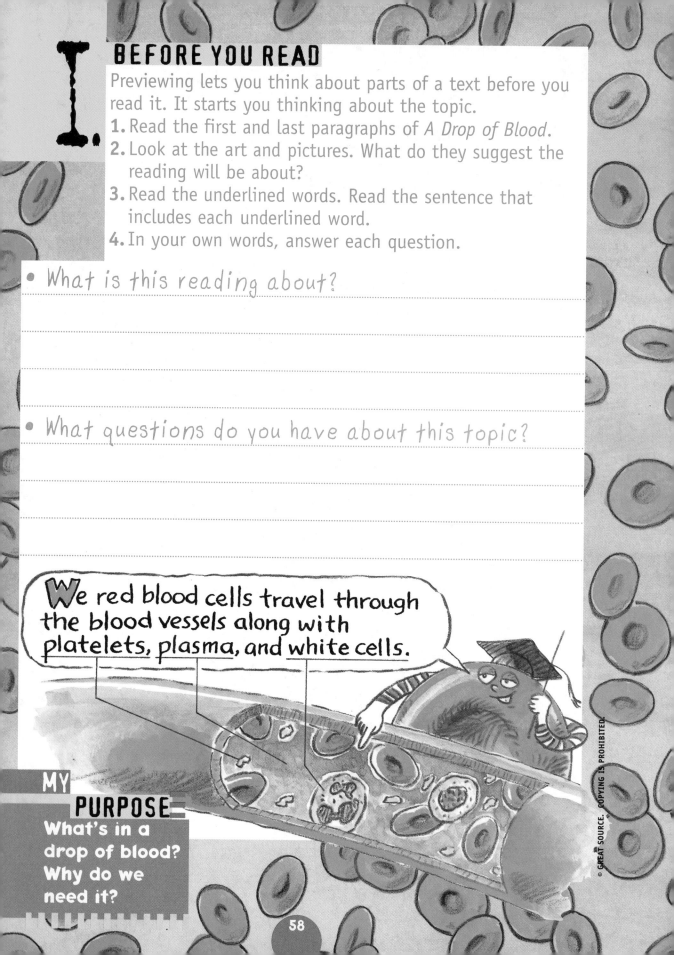

We red blood cells travel through the blood vessels along with platelets, plasma, and white cells.

MY PURPOSE

What's in a drop of blood? Why do we need it?

II. READ

Read this part of *A Drop of Blood*.
1. As you read it the first time, underline parts that tell what's in blood and why we need it.
2. Then read it again. Make pictures in your mind as you read. In the Notes, **draw** what you see.

A Drop of Blood
by Paul Showers

Blood is red because it is full of tiny red <u>cells</u>. <u>They float in a watery <u>fluid</u> called plasma.</u> The red cells are very tiny. There are hundreds—and thousands—and millions—of them in a single drop of blood.

Red cells are too small to see with your eye. You have to look at them under a <u>microscope</u>. Then the red cells look like this—round and flat, thin in the middle, thick around the edge—something like tiny doughnuts without any holes.

The blood is always moving inside your body. Your heart pumps it and keeps it moving.

cells—smallest and most basic units in a living thing.
fluid (flu•id)—liquid that flows freely.
microscope (mi•cro•scope)—instrument that makes objects that can't be seen by the eye alone large enough to see.

Response Notes

EXAMPLE:

© GREAT SOURCE. COPYING IS PROHIBITED.

59

A DROP OF BLOOD (continued)

It moves through little tubes—your blood vessels. It moves out to the tips of your fingers. It moves up to your head and down to your toes.

STOP AND THINK stop and think STOP AND

Where does blood go in your body?

STOP AND THINK STOP AND THINK STOP AND THINK

The red cells carry oxygen. Oxygen is part of the air you breathe. You cannot see oxygen, but you cannot live without it. Your body has to have oxygen every minute. You breathe oxygen into your lungs. The red cells in your blood take the oxygen from your lungs. Red cells carry the oxygen to every part of your body.

They carry oxygen to your muscles—to your bones—your brain—your stomach and intestines—your heart.

lungs—two spongelike organs that help you breathe.
stomach (stom•ach)—organ into which food passes.
intestines (in•tes•tines)—organs into which food passes from the stomach.

Why is oxygen important to people?

....

....

....

A DROP OF BLOOD (continued)

Response Notes

Your body needs food as well as oxygen.

When you eat, the food goes down to your stomach and your intestines. There food is changed into a fluid. The fluid moves from your intestines into your blood. You cannot see the food anymore, even under a microscope. But it is in your blood.

Your blood takes the food and oxygen to every part of your body. It takes food to your bones to make them grow, to your muscles to make them strong, to your fingers and your toes—even to your brain.

reread

Reread *A Drop of Blood*. As you read, think about what red blood cells do for you. Be sure you've answered the **Stop and Think** questions.

WORD WORK

A **prefix** is part of a word added to the beginning of a word. A **suffix** is part of a word added to the end of a word. Prefixes and suffixes make words longer. Adding them can also change the word's meaning.

1. Make long words by adding prefixes and suffixes to short words, which are called **base words**.
2. Write the new word in the column on the right. One has been done for you.

Prefix		Base Word		Suffix		New, Long Word
		part	+	ing	=	parting
		part	+	ed	=	
de	+	part	+	ment	=	
re	+	move	+	ed	=	
		move	+	ment	=	
un	+	move	+	able	=	

READING REMINDER

When you read about new topics, previewing and picturing ideas in your mind can help you understand new facts better.

III. GET READY TO WRITE

A. BRAINSTORM

Get ready to write an expository paragraph about red blood cells.

1. Brainstorm a list of things that red blood cells do for you.
2. One example has been done for you. Add 3–4 more things to the list.

WHAT RED BLOOD CELLS DO FOR ME

1. carry oxygen to my brain so I can think

2.

3.

4.

5.

B. ORGANIZE

Organize your paragraph into 3 parts.

1. First, complete the topic sentence.
2. Choose 3 details from your brainstorming list on page 63 that support your topic sentence.
3. Write a closing sentence that sums up what you learned about a drop of blood.

topic sentence

Red blood cells are

important because

DETAIL 1	DETAIL 2	DETAIL 3

A drop of blood

closing sentence

IV. WRITE

Now write an **expository paragraph** that tells how red blood cells can help you.

1. Begin with your topic sentence from page 64.
2. Give 3 details that support your topic sentence. Start a new sentence for each detail.
3. End with your closing sentence.
4. Use the Writers' Checklist to help you edit your paragraph.

Title:

Continue writing on the next page.

Continue your paragraph.

LOOK BACK

What made *A Drop of Blood* easy or hard to read?
Write your answer below.

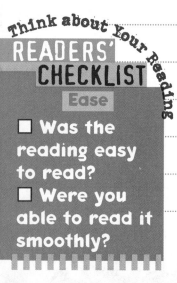

6

A River Dream

Have you ever done something that you never thought you would be able to do? How did you do it? Why did you do it?

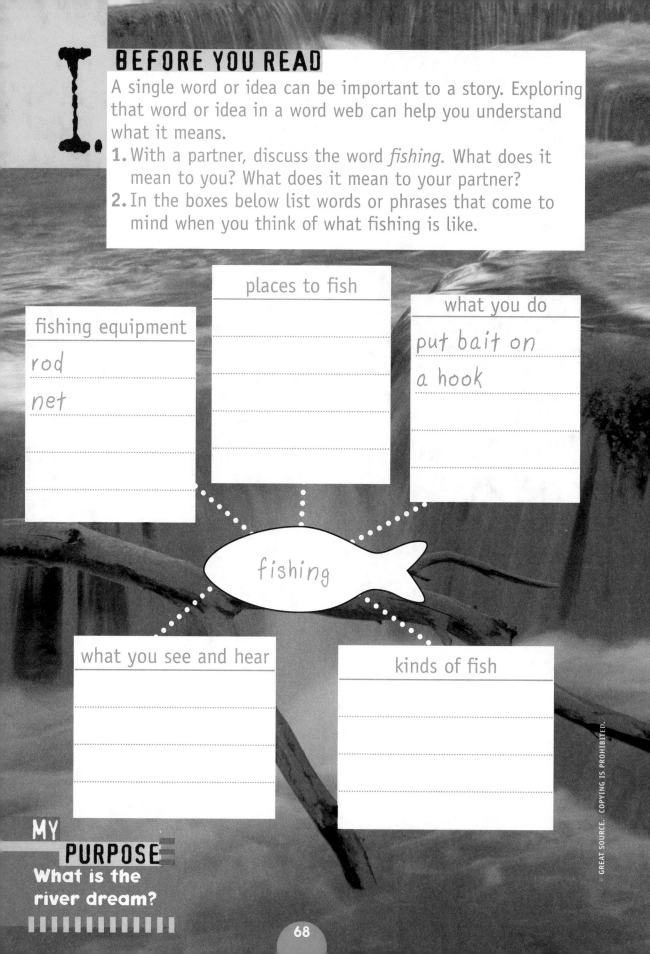

I. BEFORE YOU READ

A single word or idea can be important to a story. Exploring that word or idea in a word web can help you understand what it means.

1. With a partner, discuss the word *fishing*. What does it mean to you? What does it mean to your partner?
2. In the boxes below list words or phrases that come to mind when you think of what fishing is like.

fishing equipment
rod
net

places to fish

what you do
put bait on
a hook

fishing

what you see and hear

kinds of fish

MY PURPOSE
What is the river dream?

READ

Read this part of *A River Dream*.

1. On your first reading, underline parts that show you what Mark's river dream is.
2. On your next reading, **connect** the underlined parts to your own experiences. Write in the Notes how they make you feel.

A River Dream by Allen Say

Mark <u>flushed</u> with excitement. He raised the rod tip high, until the line hung behind his shoulder— just as his uncle had taught him. Then, with a quick, chopping stroke, he whipped the <u>rod</u> downward. The line shot out, and the cream-colored <u>fly</u> drifted down on the slick water like a snowflake. Mark took a deep breath.

flushed—turned red because of strong emotion.
rod—fishing pole.
fly—hook with feathers used to catch some kinds of fish.

Response Notes

EXAMPLE:

It seems like Mark is nervous. But he knows more about fishing than I do.

"Fine <u>cast</u>!" Uncle exclaimed. "Now keep your eye on the fly. Remember, you're not going to feel the <u>strike</u>. You're going to see it. When you see a fish take your fly, raise your rod. Easy does it, my boy, you don't want to break your line."

stop and think

Why should Mark keep watching the fly?

Mark kept his eye on the fly, and suddenly the water <u>swelled</u> under it. Then a <u>gaping</u> mouth broke the surface and the fly was gone!

"Set the hook!" Uncle shouted. Mark raised the rod, and the

cast—throw a fishing line in the water.
strike—pull on a fishing line when a fish takes the bait.
swelled—rose up.
gaping (gap•ing)—wide open.

A RIVER DREAM (continued)

rod bent over from some heavy weight. The <u>reel</u> screeched as the line ran out. A large <u>trout</u> <u>leapt</u> in the air.

STOP AND THINK **stop** and **think** STOP AND THINK

What happened when Mark raised the rod?

STOP AND THINK STOP AND THINK STOP AND THINK

"It's bigger than the one you caught!" yelled Mark.

reel—part of a fishing pole that holds the fishing line.
trout—kind of fish, often with a speckled body.
leapt—jumped upward.

"Some <u>rainbow</u>!" Uncle agreed.
"Let him <u>run</u>! Keep the rod up!"

The great trout put up a <u>mighty</u> fight, running again and again, leaping and twisting, but it could not break the line. When it could fight no more, Mark reeled it in. It barely fitted in Uncle's net.

"He's beautiful!" said Mark.

"<u>Magnificent</u>!" said Uncle. "And you're some fisherman!"

rainbow (rain•bow)—type of fish called a rainbow trout.
run—swim, pulling against the fishing line.
mighty (might•y)—powerful and strong.
Magnificent (mag•nif•i•cent)—beautiful; outstanding.

reread

Reread *A River Dream*. Think more about what the river dream was and be sure you have answered each **Stop and Think** question.

WORD WORK

Words can have more than one meaning. For example, read these sentences:

Leaves <u>fall</u> from the trees to the ground.
Leaves change color in the <u>fall</u>.

In the first sentence, <u>fall</u> is a verb that means to "go down." In the second sentence, <u>fall</u> refers to the season that occurs after summer and before winter.

1. Read each example sentence in the left-hand column.
2. Draw a line from the underlined word to its meaning on the right.

Example	Meaning
The fishing rod had a <u>fly</u>.	small insect with wings
The <u>fly</u> buzzed by my nose.	kind of fish
The <u>rainbow</u> shone in the sky.	hook used to catch fish
The <u>rainbow</u> wiggled at the end of the fishing line.	colorful reflection of light that shines in the sky after a rainfall

READING REMINDER

Reacting and connecting to characters and what they do helps you enjoy a story.

GET READY TO WRITE

A. PLAN

A River Dream tells about the steps Mark took to catch a trout. Get ready to write a paragraph about a time you did something you really wanted to do.

1. Use the storyboards below to tell your story.

2. Draw a picture in each box. Underneath, write a couple of words that describe what you've drawn.

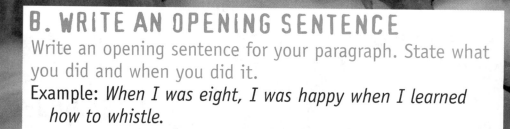

1.

2.

3.

4.

B. WRITE AN OPENING SENTENCE

Write an opening sentence for your paragraph. State what you did and when you did it.

Example: *When I was eight, I was happy when I learned how to whistle.*

My opening sentence:

IV. WRITE

Write a **narrative paragraph** about a time you did something that you really wanted to do.

1. Begin with your opening sentence and use 3–4 details from your storyboard.
2. Write a closing sentence that tells how you felt.
3. Use the Writers' Checklist to edit your paragraph.

Title:

Continue writing on the next page.

Continue your paragraph.

....

....

....

....

....

....

....

V. LOOK BACK

What would you say to a friend about *A River Dream*? Write your answer below.

....

....

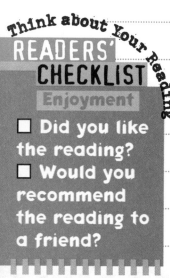

....

....

....

....

....

....

7

How We Learned the Earth Is Round

How can you tell the shape of the earth? Long ago some great thinkers asked this same question. They watched, and they thought, and they came up with an answer.

I. BEFORE YOU READ

When you read nonfiction, a K-W-L chart can help you get the most out of your reading.

1. Write in the **K** space what you think you already know about how people found out the earth was round.
2. Write what you want to find out in the **W** space. (You will fill in the **L** part later.)
3. Share what you know and what you want to learn with a partner.

K-W-L CHART

What I **K**now

What I **W**ant to Know

What I **L**earned

MY PURPOSE

How did people long ago learn that the earth was round?

READ

Read this part of *How We Learned the Earth Is Round*.

1. On your first reading, underline parts that **make clear** how people learned the earth was round.

2. On your next reading, in the Notes, sum up important facts you're learning.

How We Learned the Earth Is Round by Patricia Lauber

Today nearly everybody knows that the earth is round.

But long ago, people were <u>sure the earth was</u> flat. They thought it was flat because it looked flat. It still does.

Stand out on the <u>prairie</u>.

Sail out onto the ocean. You can see for miles, and the earth looks flat.

Climb a mountain. Now the earth looks rough and bumpy, but it doesn't seem to curve. It doesn't look round.

The earth looks flat because it is big and we are small. We see only a tiny piece at one time. The tiny piece does curve, but the curve is too

prairie (prai•rie)—flat, grassy land.

Response Notes

EXAMPLE:

A long time ago, people thought the earth was flat.

slight for our eyes to see. And that is why, for thousands of years, people thought the earth was flat.

The earth's real shape was discovered about 2,500 years ago. The people who discovered it were Greeks.

At first the Greeks, too, believed the earth was flat. But certain Greeks were great thinkers. They thought hard about things they saw and tried to explain them. They asked themselves questions—Why? What if? And then they thought some more.

Everybody knew that a strange thing happened when a ship left <u>harbor</u>. As it sailed away, it appeared to sink. First the <u>hull</u> disappeared, then the bottom of the sail, then the top.

As a ship returned, it seemed to rise out of the sea. First the sail appeared, then the hull.

The Greeks wondered why.

harbor (har•bor)—area of water near land where ships stay when they are not being used.
hull—body of a ship.

Why did people think the earth was flat?

STOP AND THINK STOP AND THINK STOP AND THINK

HOW WE LEARNED THE EARTH IS
ROUND (continued)

Response Notes

Why didn't the whole ship just get smaller and smaller or bigger and bigger? That's what should happen on a flat earth.

But it didn't happen. Why didn't it?

Perhaps the answer had to do with the shape of the earth. Perhaps the earth wasn't flat at all. Perhaps it had some other shape.

What if the earth had a curved <u>surface</u>? What would happen to a ship then?

surface (sur•face)—outer or top layer.

STOP AND THINK **stop** and **think** STOP AND THINK

What made the Greeks wonder about the shape of the earth?

You can see what happens yourself. Use a big ball and a ship made from an eraser, a toothpick, and a piece of paper. With one hand, hold the ball in front of you at eye level. Use the other hand to move the ship.

When a ship sails away over a curved surface, the bottom <u>disappears</u> first. When it returns, the top appears first.

The Greeks decided the earth must have a curved surface. That would explain why ships seemed to sink and rise.

They also saw that the same thing happened no matter which way a ship was heading—east, west, north, or south. The earth must curve in all directions.

disappears (dis•ap•**pears**)—passes out of sight.

reread

Reread *How We Learned the Earth Is Round.* On this reading, complete the **L** part of the K-W-L Chart on page 78. Be sure you have answered all the **Stop and Think** questions.

WORD WORK

Look at the word below. *Disappeared* has a prefix, a suffix, and a base word.

dis • appear • ed

prefix   *base word*   *suffix*

1. Here are some common prefixes: *dis-, re-, un-*.
2. Here are some common suffixes: *-ed, -ing*.
3. Write the prefix, base word, and suffix for each long word below. One has been done for you.

Long Words	Prefix	Base Word	Suffix
• disappeared	dis	appear	ed
• discovered			
• returning			
• reopening			
• unlearned			

READING REMINDER

Thinking about what you already know and questioning what you want to learn can help you learn more from your reading.

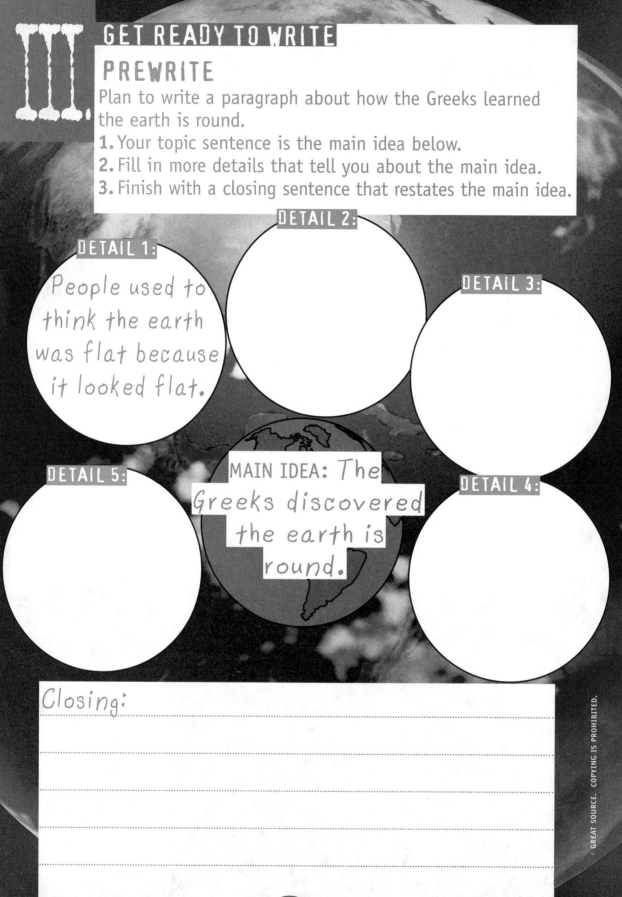

GET READY TO WRITE

PREWRITE

Plan to write a paragraph about how the Greeks learned the earth is round.

1. Your topic sentence is the main idea below.
2. Fill in more details that tell you about the main idea.
3. Finish with a closing sentence that restates the main idea.

DETAIL 2:

DETAIL 1:
People used to think the earth was flat because it looked flat.

DETAIL 3:

DETAIL 5:

MAIN IDEA: The Greeks discovered the earth is round.

DETAIL 4:

Closing:

WRITE

Write an **expository paragraph** that tells how the Greeks discovered the earth is round.

1. Begin with the main idea, the topic sentence below.
2. In the body of the paragraph, give 3 or 4 details that support your main idea.
3. End with your closing sentence.
4. Use the Writers' Checklist to help you edit your paragraph.

Title:

The Greeks discovered the earth is round.

Continue your writing on the next page.

Continue your paragraph.

....

....

....

....

....

....

....

....

LOOK BACK

What is *How We Learned the Earth Is Round* about?
Write your answer below in your own words.

....

....

....

....

....

....

8

I Am Rosa Parks

What do you do when you think a rule isn't fair? Do you yell? Do you cry? Do you write a letter? What other things could you do?

BEFORE YOU READ

A preview helps you look ahead. It helps you focus on what you know about the topic.

1. First, read the title. What will this reading be about?
2. Second, read the first and last paragraphs.
3. Read the underlined words and study the pictures. Finally, answer these questions.

PREVIEWING QUESTIONS

1. What do you think the topic is?

2. Who do you think Rosa Parks is?

3. What do you predict her story will be about?

MY PURPOSE

Who is Rosa Parks, and what did she do that made her famous?

READ

Read this part of *I Am Rosa Parks*.

1. On your first reading, circle parts of the story that help you understand who Rosa Parks was.
2. On your next reading, write **questions** you have about her and her life in the Notes.

I Am Rosa Parks
by Rosa Parks

Many years ago (black people) in the South could not go to the same schools as white people. (We) could not eat in white restaurants. We could not even drink from the same water fountains.

We had to stay apart from white people everywhere we went. This was called segregation. Segregation was the law in the South. If we broke the law, we could be <u>arrested</u>, or hurt, or even killed.

arrested (ar•rest•ed)—held by the police for breaking the law.

Response Notes

EXAMPLE:

Why couldn't they eat in white restaurants?

DINER

WHITE ONLY

89

Write the effect that comes from the cause sentence.

Cause:	Effect:
A black person breaks a law.	

Response Notes

I AM ROSA PARKS (continued)

When we rode a bus, we could only sit in the back seats. The front seats were just for white people.

If all the front seats were filled by white people, we black people had to give up our seats for the next white people who got on the bus.

That's the way we rode buses in the South when I was younger. I rode the buses and <u>obeyed</u> the laws that kept me apart from white people. But I did not think they were right.

obeyed (o•beyed)—followed a law or order.

I AM ROSA PARKS (continued)

One day I was riding on a bus. I was sitting in one of the seats in the back section for black people. The bus started to get crowded. The front seats filled up with white people. One white man was standing up.

The bus driver looked back at us black people sitting down.

cause ▶ and ◀ effect

Write the effect that comes from the cause sentence.

Cause:	Effect:
The seats were filled, and one white man was standing.	

The driver said, "Let me have those seats." He wanted us to get up and give our seats to white people. But I was tired of doing that. I stayed in my seat. The bus driver said to me, "I'm going to have you arrested."

"You may do that," I said. And I stayed in my seat.

Two policemen came. One asked me, "Why didn't you stand up?"

I asked him, "Why do you push us black people around?"

cause and effect

Write the effect that comes from the cause sentence.

Cause:	Effect:
Rosa wouldn't give up her seat.	

reread

Reread *I Am Rosa Parks*. As you do, think more about what Rosa Parks did. Be sure you have written an effect that comes from each cause.

WORD WORK

If you can read one word, it's easy to read a word that's almost the same.

Say *ride*. Now take off the *r* and put *str* in front of *ide*. The new word is *stride*.

Use the letters in the box to build new words. These letters are single consonants (such as *c, b, m*) and consonant clusters (such as *bl, st, sp*).

Letters

| d m b t |

Clusters

| fl   tr   bl   sm   st   cr   sp |

1. Make 3 new words for each word listed below. You can use clusters or single letters from the boxes above.
2. The first one has been done for you.

1. back	black	track	tack
2. jail			
3. seat			
4. send			
5. park			

READING REMINDER

Asking questions as you read helps you stay interested and involved in what you're reading.

GET READY TO WRITE

CREATE A WEB

Think about what Rosa Parks was like as a person. What did she do or say? How would you describe her in a letter to a friend? Fill in the web below with details from the reading that show what Rosa was like.

HOW WAS SHE BRAVE?

She stayed in her seat when the bus driver said, "Let me have those seats."

HOW WAS SHE PEACEFUL?

HOW WAS SHE STUBBORN?   (Rosa Parks)   **HOW WAS SHE FAIR?**

WRITE

Now you are ready to write your own **letter**. Write to a friend about who Rosa Parks was.

1. Use details from your web on the previous page.
2. Use the Writers' Checklist to edit your letter.

Continue writing on the next page.

Continue your letter.

....

....

....

....

....

....

....

....

....

....

V. LOOK BACK

What 2 things did you learn from *I Am Rosa Parks*?
Write your answer below.

....

....

....

....

....

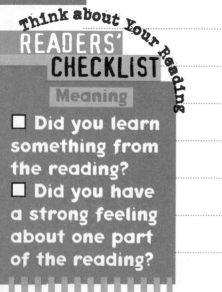

9

Germs Make Me Sick!

Have you ever felt like you couldn't get out of bed? You have a headache, your throat is sore, and your nose is stuffy. People get sick, but how?

With a reading partner, take turns reading the sentences below from *Germs Make Me Sick!*

1. Check the box to show whether you agree or disagree.

2. Share your opinions with your partner.

agree	disagree	
☐	☐	Germs are what make you sick.
☐	☐	You can see a germ with your eyes.
☐	☐	Germs are in the air you breathe.
☐	☐	All germs make you sick.
☐	☐	You can't get germs from sharing a glass of water.

3. Make a prediction about what *Germs Make Me Sick!* will be about.

My prediction:

MY PURPOSE

What are germs, and how can they make people sick?

READ

Read *Germs Make Me Sick!*

1. As you read it the first time, underline parts that **make clear** what germs are and how they can make people sick.
2. As you read it a second time, write in the Notes any facts you're learning about germs.

Germs Make Me Sick!
by Melvin Berger

You wake up one morning. But you don't feel like getting out of bed. Your arms and legs <u>ache</u>. Your head hurts. You have a fever. And your <u>throat</u> is sore.

"I'm sick," you say. "I must have caught a germ."

Everyone knows that germs can make you sick. But not everyone knows how.

<u>Germs are tiny living things.</u> They are far too small to see with your eyes alone. In fact, a line of one thousand germs could fit across the top of a pencil!

There are many different kinds

ache—hurt with a dull, long-lasting pain.
throat—passage that leads from the mouth to the stomach.

Response Notes

EXAMPLE:

Germs are too small to see.

© GREAT SOURCE. COPYING IS PROHIBITED.

of germs. But the two that usually make you sick are <u>bacteria</u> and <u>viruses</u>.

Under a microscope, some bacteria look like little round balls. Others are as straight as rods. Still others are twisted in <u>spiral</u> shapes.

Viruses are far tinier than bacteria. Some look like balls with spikes sticking out on all sides. Others look like loaves of bread or like <u>tadpoles</u>. There are even some that look like metal screws with spider legs.

RETELL RETELL RETELL **retell** RETELL RETELL RETELL

How are viruses different from bacteria?

RETELL RETELL RETELL RETELL RETELL RETELL

Germs, such as bacteria and viruses, are found everywhere. They are in the air you breathe, in

bacteria (bac•te•ri•a)—one-celled organisms.
viruses (vi•rus•es)—things that cause disease.
spiral (spi•ral)—shaped like a circle or coiled.
tadpoles (tad•poles)—baby frogs.

GERMS MAKE ME SICK! (continued)

the food you eat, in the water you drink, and on everything you touch. They are even on your skin and in your body.

Although germs are all around, they do not always make you sick. Many germs are not <u>harmful</u>. Also, your body keeps out harmful germs most of the time.

Your skin blocks the germs. As long as there are no cuts or scratches on your skin, germs can't get in.

Your nose helps, too. It is <u>lined</u> with tiny hairs. The hairs catch many of the germs you breathe in. They push them back out.

The inside of your mouth and throat is always wet. Germs often get stuck there. They don't go any further.

harmful (harm•ful)—able to hurt you.
lined—covered on the inside.

RETELL RETELL retell RETELL RETELL RETELL

What 2 parts of the body help keep germs out of you?

Yet some germs do slip in every once in a while.

Your friend has a cold. She sneezes. Germs fly out. You breathe the air. Some of her germs may get into your lungs.

You take a sip of your cousin's soda. Her germs are on the straw. A few of the germs may get into your stomach.

You're riding a bike. You fall and <u>scrape</u> your knee. Germs from the ground may get under your skin.

But even when harmful bacteria and viruses get into your body, you don't always get sick. That is because your body has ways to fight germs.

scrape—scratch; rub some skin off.

RETELL RETELL RETELL **retell** RETELL RETELL RETELL

What are 3 ways germs can get inside of you?

reread

Reread *Germs Make Me Sick!* Pay attention to what you learned about germs. Be sure you have answered the **Retell** questions.

WORD WORK

Sometimes a long word is made by joining 2 short words. The long word is called a **compound word**.

Short Word		Short Word		Compound Word
every	+	one	=	everyone

1. Look back at *Germs Make Me Sick!*
2. Find 3 compound words in this selection.
3. Write the compound words below and complete the chart.

Compound Word	Short Word	Short Word
1.		
2.		
3.		

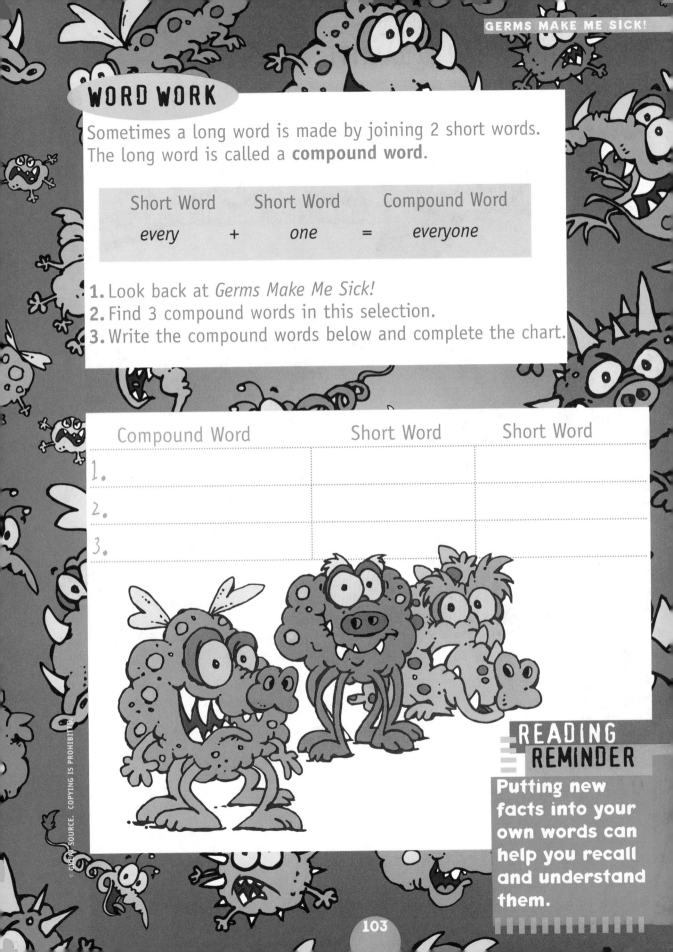

READING REMINDER

Putting new facts into your own words can help you recall and understand them.

III.

GET READY TO WRITE

A. ASK QUESTIONS

What did you learn about germs? Show what you know on this chart.

1. WHAT ARE GERMS?

2. HOW DO GERMS MAKE ME SICK?

MY TOPIC

Germs make me sick.

3. WHY DO GERMS MAKE ME SICK?

5. WHO CAN CATCH GERMS?

4. WHERE ARE GERMS?

B. PLAN

Get ready to write a paragraph that explains what you've learned about germs. Before you start, write what your topic sentence will be. It should tell what your paragraph is going to be about.

My topic sentence:

IV. WRITE

Write an **expository paragraph** that answers some of the questions in the web on the previous page.

1. Start with your topic sentence.
2. Choose 3–4 details from the web. Write a separate sentence for each detail.
3. In the closing sentence, tell how you feel about germs.
4. Use the Writers' Checklist to edit your paragraph.

Title:

Continue writing on the next page.

Continue your paragraph.

....

....

....

....

....

....

....

....

V. LOOK BACK

What would you tell someone *Germs Make Me Sick!* is about? Write your answer below.

....

....

....

....

....

....

The Skirt

Have you ever made a mistake?
How did it make you feel?
In the story *The Skirt*,
Miata makes a terrible
mistake. Can she
correct it?

BEFORE YOU READ

To start thinking before you read, preview *The Skirt*.
1. First, look at the pictures.
2. Next, read the first and the last paragraphs.
3. Let your eyes go over each page and then answer the questions below.

Why do you think Miata wants to catch the bus?

Why is the skirt important to Miata?

MY
PURPOSE
Why is the skirt so important to Miata? What is her problem?

II.

READ

Read this part of *The Skirt*.

1. On your first reading, circle parts of the story that tell you about Miata's problem and why the skirt is important to her.

2. Then read it a second time. In your Notes, **connect** Miata's problem to experiences and feelings you've had.

The Skirt by Gary Soto

"Please stop!" Miata yelled as she ran after the bus. Her legs kicked high and her lungs burned from <u>exhaustion</u>.

She needed that skirt. On Sunday after church she was ⟨going to dance⟩ <u>folklórico</u>. Her <u>troupe</u> had practiced for three months. If she was the only girl without a costume, her parents would wear sunglasses out of embarrassment. Miata didn't want that.

Response Notes

EXAMPLE:

I wore the wrong outfit once.

exhaustion (ex•**haus**•tion)—being extremely tired and worn out.
folklórico (folk•**ló**•ri•co)—kind of folk dance.
troupe—group of performers.

The skirt had belonged to her mother when she was a child in Hermosillo, Mexico. What is Mom going to think? Miata asked herself. Her mother was always <u>scolding</u> Miata for losing things. She lost combs, sweaters, books, lunch money, and homework. One time she even lost her shoes at school. She had left them on the baseball field where she had raced against two boys. When she returned to get them, the shoes were gone.

scolding (scold•ing)—finding fault with or blaming.

stop and think

Why is Miata worried?

THE SKIRT (continued)

Worse, she had taken her skirt to school to show off. She wanted her friends to see it. The skirt was old, but a rainbow of shiny ribbons still made it pretty. She put it on during lunchtime and danced for some of her friends. Even a teacher stopped to watch.

What am I going to do now? Miata asked herself. She slowed to a walk. Her hair had come undone. She felt hot and sticky.

She could hear the bus stopping around the corner. Miata thought of running through a neighbor's yard. But that would only get her in trouble.

STOP AND THINK **stop** and **think** STOP AND THINK

What do you think Miata should do?

"Oh, man," Miata said under her breath. She felt like throwing herself on the ground and crying. But she knew that would only make things worse. Her mother would ask, "Why do you get so dirty all the time?"

Miata turned the corner and saw a paper plane sail from the <u>rear</u> window. It hung in the air for a second and then crashed into a <u>ragged</u> rosebush as the bus drove off. She carefully <u>plucked</u> the plane from the bush. When she unfolded it she discovered Rodolfo's math quiz. He had a perfect score. A gold star glittered under his name.

"He's smart," she said. "For a boy."

rear—back.
ragged (rag•ged)—not perfect; damaged and rough.
plucked—removed with a quick pull.

THE SKIRT (continued)

She crumpled the paper plane and looked up. The bus was now out of sight. So was her beautiful skirt.

reread

Read *The Skirt* again. Think again what Miata's problem was and why the skirt was important to her. Make sure you have answered all the **Stop and Think** questions.

WORD WORK

You can build long words by combining a word part, such as *auto-*, with small words and other word parts.

auto- + matic = *automatic*   auto- + graph = *autograph*

Complete the web below by adding *auto-* to words and word parts in the box below.

WORD AND WORD PARTS BOX

graph	mobile	motive	mated	mation

auto
means by itself
or self-moving

READING REMINDER

Previewing helps you start thinking about the story so that you understand it more easily.

III. GET READY TO WRITE

A. ORGANIZE

Use the chart below to organize your thoughts about *The Skirt*.

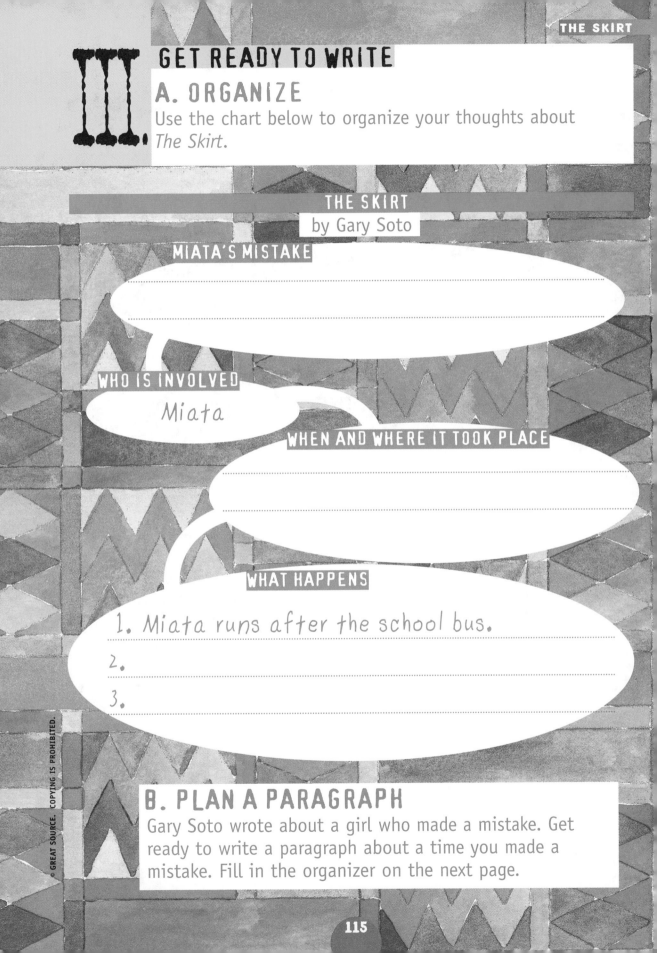

THE SKIRT
by Gary Soto

MIATA'S MISTAKE

WHO IS INVOLVED
Miata

WHEN AND WHERE IT TOOK PLACE

WHAT HAPPENS

1. *Miata runs after the school bus.*
2.
3.

B. PLAN A PARAGRAPH

Gary Soto wrote about a girl who made a mistake. Get ready to write a paragraph about a time you made a mistake. Fill in the organizer on the next page.

MY PARAGRAPH

MISTAKE

....
....
....

WHO WAS INVOLVED

....
....

WHEN AND WHERE IT TOOK PLACE

....
....
....
....

WHAT HAPPENED

1. ....
....
2. ....
....
3. ....
....

 **WRITE**

Write a **narrative paragraph**. Describe a time that you made a mistake.

1. Begin with a topic sentence that tells the problem and how you felt.
2. Use what you wrote on page 116 to help you tell about the mistake you made.
3. Use the Writers' Checklist to edit your paragraph.

Title:

Continue writing on the next page.

Continue your paragraph.

....

....

....

....

....

....

....

....

V. LOOK BACK

What about Miata's story did you like the most? Why? Write your answer below.

....

....

....

....

Through Grandpa's Eyes

Have you ever gotten up in the middle of the night and it was so dark you could not see? How did you get around? Did you put your hands out in front of you? Sometimes not being able to see lets you see even more.

BEFORE YOU READ

Predicting keeps you wondering what the story is about.

1. Think about the title *Through Grandpa's Eyes*.
2. Study the pictures.
3. Read the 4 sentences from the story.
4. Number them in the order you think they come in the story.

☐ "When he eats, Grandpa's plate of food is a clock."

☐ "But Grandpa's house is my favorite."

☐ "And his eyes are sharp blue even though they are not sharp seeing."

☐ "I walk behind him, my fingers following Grandpa's smooth path."

5. Now, make a prediction. What do you think this story will be about?

My prediction:

....

....

....

....

MY PURPOSE
Why are Grandpa and his house so special?

I. READ

Read this part of *Through Grandpa's Eyes*.
1. Highlight details that describe Grandpa and his house.
2. Read it a second time and think about what Grandpa and his house may look like. In the Notes, **draw** pictures of what you "see" in your mind.

Through Grandpa's Eyes
by Patricia MacLachlan

Of all the houses that I know, I like my grandpa's best. My friend Peter has a new glass house with <u>pebble-path</u> gardens that go nowhere. And Maggie lives next door in an old wooden house with rooms behind rooms, all with <u>carved</u> doors and <u>brass</u> doorknobs. They are fine houses. But Grandpa's house is my favorite. Because I see it through Grandpa's eyes.

Grandpa is <u>blind</u>. He doesn't see the house the way I do. He has his own way of seeing.

In the morning, the sun pushes through the curtains into my eyes.

pebble-path (peb•ble path)—walkway made out of small stones.
carved—decorated by making cuttings in the wood.
brass—yellowish metal.
blind—not able to see.

Response Notes

EXAMPLE:

I <u>burrow</u> down into the covers to get away, but the light follows me. I give up, throw back the covers, and run to Grandpa's room. The sun wakes Grandpa differently from the way it wakes me. He says it touches him, *warming* him awake. When I peek around the door, Grandpa is already up and doing his morning exercises. Bending and stretching by the bed. He stops and smiles because he hears me.

RETELL RETELL RETELL **retell** RETELL RETELL

How does the sun wake up Grandpa?

RETELL RETELL RETELL RETELL RETELL RETELL RETELL

"Good morning, John."
"Where's Nana?" I ask him.
"Don't you know?" he says, bending and stretching. "Close your eyes, John, and look through my eyes."

burrow (bur•row)—hide, like an animal going into a tunnel.

THROUGH GRANDPA'S EYES (continued)

I close my eyes. Down below, I hear the banging of pots and the sound of water running that I didn't hear before.

"Nana is in the kitchen, making breakfast," I say.

When I open my eyes again, I can see Grandpa nodding at me. He is tall with dark gray hair. And his eyes are <u>sharp</u> blue even though they are not sharp seeing.

RETELL RETELL RETELL RETELL RETELL RETELL RETELL

What does Grandpa teach John to do?

RETELL RETELL RETELL RETELL RETELL RETELL RETELL

I exercise with Grandpa. Up and down. Then I try to exercise with my eyes closed.

"One, two," says Grandpa, "three, four."

"Wait!" I cry. I am still on one, two when Grandpa is on three, four.

I fall sideways. Three times. Grandpa laughs as he hears

one Two

Three Four

sharp—clear and distinct.

my thumps on the carpet.

"Breakfast!" calls Nana from downstairs.

"I smell eggs frying," says Grandpa. He bends his head close to mine. "And buttered toast."

The wooden <u>banister</u> on the stairway has been worn smooth from Grandpa running his fingers up and down. I walk behind him, my fingers following Grandpa's smooth path.

We go into the kitchen.

"I smell flowers," says Grandpa.

"What flowers?" I ask.

He smiles. He loves guessing games.

"Not violets, John, not peonies ..."

"Carnations!" I cry. I love guessing games.

"Silly." Grandpa laughs. "Marigolds. Right, Nana?"

Nana laughs, too.

"That's too easy," she says, putting two plates of food in front of us.

"It's not too easy," I <u>protest</u>.

banister (ban•is•ter)—handrail of a staircase.
protest (pro•test)—object or argue.

THROUGH GRANDPA'S EYES (continued)

"How can Grandpa tell? All the smells mix together in the air."

"Close your eyes, John," says Nana. "Tell me what breakfast is."

"I smell the eggs. I smell the toast," I say, my eyes closed. "And something else. The something else doesn't smell good."

"*That* something else," says Nana, smiling, "is the marigolds."

When he eats, Grandpa's plate of food is a clock.

"Two eggs at nine o'clock and toast at two o'clock," says Nana to Grandpa. "And a <u>dollop</u> of jam."

"A dollop of jam," I tell Grandpa, "at six o'clock."

I make my plate of food a clock, too, and eat through Grandpa's eyes.

dollop (dol•lop)—lump or portion.

reread

Reread *Through Grandpa's Eyes*. Look again at the details that help you understand what Grandpa and his house are like. Be sure you have answered the **Retell** questions.

WORD WORK

Words have beats—1, 2, 3, or more beats. Try clapping *grandpa*. You clapped 2 times because *grand•pa* has 2 beats called **syllables**.

Some 2-syllable words have consonant letters in the middle. These letters can be the same consonants (pe<u>bb</u>le), or the letters can be 2 different consonants (cur<u>t</u>ains).

WORD BOX

finger	burrow	morning	ladder
running	breakfast	nodded	

1. Put the words with the same consonants in the middle in the left-hand column.
2. Put the words with 2 different consonants in the right-hand column.
3. Put a line between the consonants to divide each word. One has been done for you.

Same Consonant Letters	Different Consonant Letters
bur/row	

GET READY TO WRITE

A. PICK A TOPIC

In *Through Grandpa's Eyes*, John begins to pay attention to what he hears, smells, and feels—not just what he sees. Get ready to describe a room in your home or your school that makes your senses come alive.

1. Close your eyes and "see" the room in your mind.
2. Write details in each part of the web below.

WHAT I HEAR

WHAT I SEE

WHAT I SMELL

WHAT I TASTE

My Special Room

WHAT I TOUCH

B. DESCRIBE A PLACE

Plan your paragraph. Write sentences that describe your special room.

1. Choose 1 detail from each box on page 127 to put in each of the small boxes below.
2. Write a sentence that uses each detail.

WHAT I SEE

WHAT I HEAR

WHAT I TOUCH

WHAT I TASTE

WHAT I SMELL

IV. WRITE

Write a **descriptive paragraph** about a room.

1. Begin by filling in the topic sentence below.
2. Use your notes from page 128 to give 3–4 different sense details to describe the room. Start a new sentence for each detail.
3. Write a closing sentence that tells how you feel about the room.
4. Use the Writers' Checklist to edit your paragraph.

Title: ....

↓NAME OF ROOM↓

When I walk into _____,

my senses come alive.

Continue writing on the next page.

Continue your paragraph.

....

....

....

....

....

....

....

....

V. LOOK BACK

How would you describe *Through Grandpa's Eyes* to a friend? Write your answer below.

....

....

....

....

....

....

12

Me and My Shadow

Was there a moon last night?
What did it look like? What
will it look like tomorrow?
The moon seems to
change size, but
what is really
happening?

BEFORE YOU READ

Get ready to read about shadows and the moon.

1. Get together with a reading partner.
2. Read each sentence below and mark whether you agree or disagree.
3. Share your answers with your reading partner.

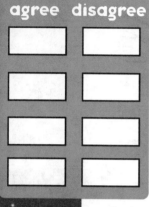

agree	disagree	
☐	☐	A huge shadow gives us day and night.
☐	☐	When the earth is in the shadow, we have night.
☐	☐	The moon has a shadow.
☐	☐	The moon circles the earth.

4. Make a prediction about what *Me and My Shadow* will be about.

My prediction: _____

_____

_____

_____

_____

MY PURPOSE

What are shadows, and what do they have to do with the moon?

READ

Read this part of *Me and My Shadow*.

1. On your first reading, underline parts that give you important details about shadows and the moon.
2. Read through the selection again. In the Notes, write **questions** you have about shadows.

Me and My Shadow
by Arthur Dorros

Response Notes

There are shadows all around us. A <u>gigantic</u> shadow is what gives us day and night. The earth is like a big ball that spins in space. As our part of the earth spins toward the sun, we have day. When our <u>part of the earth is in the shadow, we have night.</u>

EXAMPLE:

How many miles long is the shadow?

stop and organize

What things have you learned about day and night?

STOP AND ORGANIZE STOP AND ORGANIZE

You can see how this happens. Shine a flashlight on a ball in a dark room. On the side of the ball that is away from the light there is

gigantic (gi•**gan**•tic)—very big.

a shadow. On this side, it is nighttime.

The moon has a shadow too. The moon <u>circles</u> the earth. One half of the moon always faces the sun. It is lit up. The side away from the sun is always dark. It is the shadow side of the moon.

The moon takes many days and nights to circle the earth. Each night, depending on where the moon is in its circle around the earth, we see a different amount of the moon's shadow and its lit-up side.

circles (cir•cles)—moves around.

stop and organize

What have you learned about the moon?

ME AND MY SHADOW (continued)

On this night, the moon looks like just a <u>sliver</u>. That is because we are seeing more of the moon's shadow and less of the lit-up side than on other nights. On nights that the moon looks round and full, we are seeing more of the lit-up side and less shadow.

sliver (sliv•er)—small, narrow piece.

reread

Reread *Me and My Shadow*. Think again about what shadows have to do with the moon. Be sure you have answered the **Stop and Organize** questions.

WORD WORK

You can build **compound words** by combining 2 small words. The word *moon* is used often in *Me and My Shadow*.

1. Choose from the small words in the box below to make 3 more compound words that start with *moon*.
2. One has been done for you.

WORD BOX

moon +

light	beam	stop	move
shine	fish	rise	walk

=

1. moonwalk
2.
3.
4.

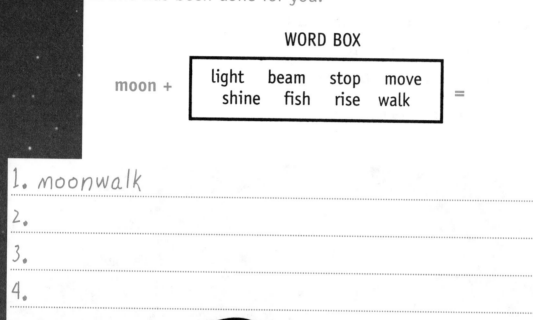

READING REMINDER

Asking questions when you read nonfiction helps you relate new information to what you already know.

III. GET READY TO WRITE
A. ORGANIZE YOUR THOUGHTS
Fill in 3 more details that tell you about the main idea below.

MAIN IDEA

Shadows are all around us.

DETAIL #1

When our part of the earth spins toward the sun, we have day.

DETAIL #2

DETAIL #3

DETAIL #4

When the moon looks like a sliver, we are seeing a lot of shadow.

DETAIL #5

B. BRAINSTORM

Get ready to write a poem about shadows using some of the facts you've learned.

1. Brainstorm a list of words that remind you of the word *shadow*. Three have been done for you.
2. Look back in the story to get some ideas.

BRAINSTORM LIST—SHADOW

silent   night   sun

WRITE

Write a **poem** about shadows.
1. Give your poem a title.
2. Use the line starters below to write your own poem.
3. Add words you wrote on page 138 to help you complete the lines.
4. Use the Writers' Checklist to edit your poem.

Title: ....

A Shadow is ....

....

It ....

....

Sometimes ....

....

Other times ....

....

Once ....

....

Continue writing on the next page.

Continue your poem.

I wish

....

....

....

I wonder

....

....

....

 **LOOK BACK**

What information was easy for you to remember about shadows? What was hard? Write your answer below.

....

....

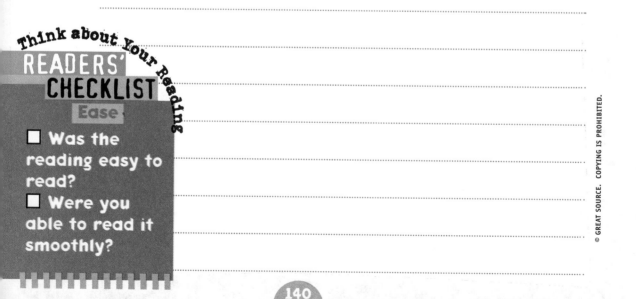

13

Follow That Trash!

Have you ever wondered what happens to all the paper and leftover lunches kids in your school throw out each day? Find out about the different ways people get rid of garbage.

BEFORE YOU READ

Get ready to read about trash and what happens to it.

1. With a reading partner, read each statement.
2. Write "True" in the space if you think the statement is true.
3. Write "False" in the space if you think the statement is false.

.... You throw out about 4 pounds of garbage a day.

.... It's easy to get rid of everyone's trash.

.... Some trash is burned.

.... Most trash is buried in the ground.

4. Now answer the question below and share your ideas with a reading partner.

What do you think you will learn by reading *Follow That Trash!*?

....
....
....
....
....
....

MY PURPOSE
What happens to garbage after it is thrown out?

II. READ

Read this part of *Follow That Trash!*

1. The first time you read it, highlight parts of *Follow That Trash!* that **make clear** what happens to garbage after we throw it away.

2. Then read it a second time. In the Notes, write in your own words some of the facts you're learning.

Follow That Trash!
by Francine Jacobs

Every day you throw out about four pounds of trash.

So does everybody else in America!

In a year that's 180 million tons—enough to fill a line of garbage trucks halfway to the moon.

But after you put out your trash, what happens to it?

Getting rid of garbage is a problem. Most trash is buried in places called landfills. But landfills fill up. They are ugly and dangerous, too. Some <u>leak</u> <u>poisons</u> that <u>pollute</u> our water. Yuck! Who

leak—let a substance escape.
poisons (poi•sons)—stuff that causes people to get sick or die.
pollute (pol•lute)—make unhealthy for living things.

Response Notes

EXAMPLE:
A lot of trash goes into landfills.

wants to drink water that can make you sick? Some people are trying to pass laws to stop landfills.

DOUBLE-ENTRY JOURNAL

Quote	My Thoughts About It
"But landfills fill up. They are ugly and dangerous, too."	

Trash is also burned in <u>incinerators</u>. (You say it like this: in-SIN-er-a-tors.) Incinerators make lots of smoke. Some of the smoke is poisonous. Pee-U! No one wants to breathe that smelly stuff! Burning trash also makes <u>soot</u> and <u>ashes</u>. Soot makes our

incinerators (in•cin•er•a•tors)—places that burn trash.
soot—black particles formed by burning.
ashes (ash•es)—white or black substances left behind after something is burned.

FOLLOW THAT TRASH! (continued)

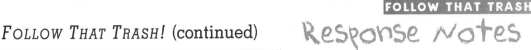

Response Notes

clothes dirty, and our faces, too! People don't want incinerators where they live. Would you?

DOUBLE-ENTRY JOURNAL

Quote	My Thoughts About It
"People don't want incinerators where they live. Would you?"	

green glass   brown glass   Paper   Plastic   aluminum cans   other metal

Is there a better way to get rid of trash? There sure is! Recycling!

Recycling means turning things that have been used into new things. Much of the trash we throw away can be recycled.

← ← ← ← reread ← ← ←

Read *Follow That Trash!* again. Think about what you've learned about garbage after it is thrown out. Be sure you have written in the **Double-entry Journals.**

WORD WORK

A number of words end in a consonant letter before a final *y*. Take, for example, *try* or *lazy*. These words are tricky because the *y* changes to an *i* when you add a suffix or ending that starts with a vowel. This can make them hard to read.

try + -ed = *tried*   lazy + -er = *lazier*

1. Add suffixes to the words below.
2. Remember to change the *y* to an *i* and then add the suffix. One has been done for you.

Word	+ er	+ est
• dry	drier	driest
• easy		
• noisy		
• busy		
• creepy		

READING REMINDER

Talking about a topic with a partner before you read can help you get more out of your reading.

III. GET READY TO WRITE

A. SUPPORT YOUR OPINION

Get ready to write a paragraph of opinion. Think about this opinion statement: It's important to recycle our trash.

1. Under the statement below, fill in the details.
2. It may help to look through the reading again as you're answering the questions.

Opinion Statement: It's important to recycle our trash.

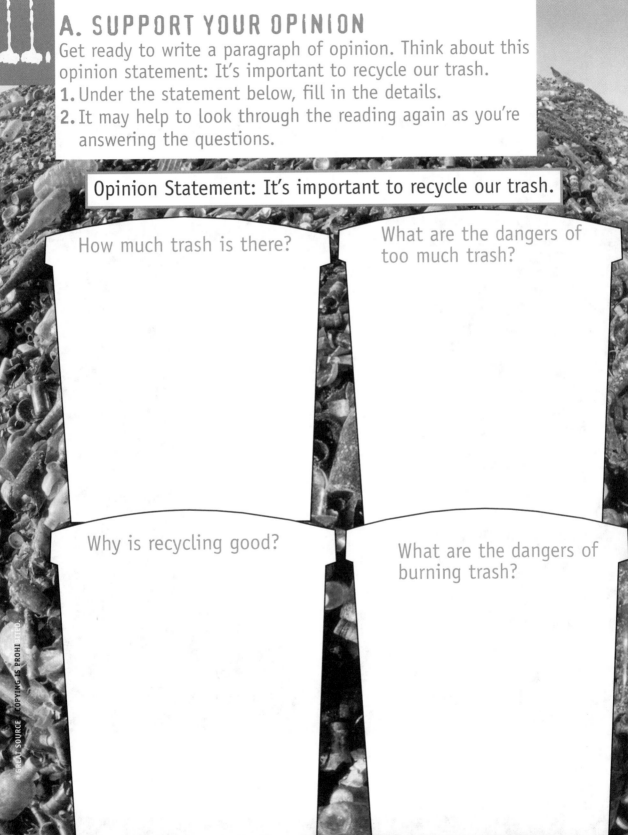

How much trash is there?

What are the dangers of too much trash?

Why is recycling good?

What are the dangers of burning trash?

B. STUDY A MODEL

A paragraph has 3 basic parts: a topic sentence, supporting details, and a closing sentence.

1. Study the model of a paragraph below.
2. Use it to help you write your paragraph of opinion about the importance of recycling trash.

Topic Sentence
Nobody wants to live with trash all around.

Supporting Details

In my family alone, we make twelve pounds of trash a day.

Trash not only looks bad, but it can poison us.

Leaking landfills can cause water pollution.

Burning trash creates smoke, which is bad for us.

Closing Sentence
My belief is that too much trash will harm us, so we should recycle.

WRITE

Write a **paragraph of opinion** about why recycling trash is important. Use the model on page 148 to help you.

1. Open with the opinion statement from page 147. That is your topic sentence.
2. Support your topic sentence with ideas from your chart on page 147.
3. Close your paragraph by stating why you are in favor of recycling.
4. Use the Writers' Checklist to edit your paragraph.

Title:

Continue writing on the next page.

Continue your paragraph.

....

....

....

....

....

....

....

....

V. LOOK BACK

What are 2 things you learned about trash? Write your answer below.

....

....

....

....

....

....

....

14

Otherwise Known as Sheila the Great

You're in bed. The lights
are out. It's darker than
night. You hear creeek,
creeeeek, creeeek.
What are you
going to do?

BEFORE YOU READ

How do you get ready to read a story? One way is to look through it.

1. Read the title and first paragraph.
2. Look at the pictures and notice names of characters. Then read a few sentences from the story.
3. Put a number in front of each sentence, telling the order you think it appears in the story.
4. Then make a prediction.

	"That's when I saw the spider."
	"I jumped out of bed and ran down the hall to my parents' room."
	"I heard this really scary noise."

I predict the story will be about

....
....
....
....
....
....
....

MY PURPOSE

What happens to Sheila the Great, and what is she scared about?

READ

Read this part of *Otherwise Known As Sheila the Great.*

1. On your first reading, underline parts of the story that explain what is happening to Sheila and why she is scared.

2. Then, as you read it a second time, **connect** what happens to Sheila to experiences and feelings you've had. Write your thoughts in the Notes.

Otherwise Known As Sheila the Great by Judy Blume

I got into bed. My room was very dark. I'm not used to sleeping all by myself in the dark. I closed my eyes but nothing happened. So I got out of bed and turned on the light. That was a little better. Soon the house was quiet. <u>I knew everyone else was sound asleep</u>. I tossed around for a while. Then I tried lying on my back. I looked up at the <u>ceiling</u>. I tried to think of something funny. Something that would give me a good dream.

sound asleep (sound a•sleep)—in a deep sleep.
ceiling (ceil•ing)—top part of a room.

Response Notes

EXAMPLE:
I don't like being awake when everyone else in the house is asleep.

!!*!*!* stop and organize *!*!*!*!*

What is the setting of this story?

Where?

When?

Response Notes

OTHERWISE KNOWN AS SHEILA THE GREAT (continued)

That's when I saw the spider. He was running across my ceiling. I hate spiders! One time Peter Hatcher put a fake spider in my desk at school. When I took out my English book, there it was. But I knew it was a <u>phony</u> right away. So I held it by one leg and took it up to Mrs. Haver. "Just look what Peter Hatcher put inside my desk," I said, shaking the spider.

Mrs. Haver screamed so loud she scared the whole class. And Peter Hatcher had to stay after school for three days!

I looked at my ceiling again. The spider was still there and *this* one was no phony. "Go away,

phony (pho•ny)—fake; not real.

OTHERWISE KNOWN AS SHEILA THE
GREAT (continued)

spider!" I whispered. "Please go away and don't come back." But the spider didn't move. He was right over my head. Suppose he falls on me, I thought. Suppose he's the <u>poisonous</u> kind and when he falls he bites me. Maybe I should put my head under the covers. Then if he falls on me it won't matter. No, that's no good either. He could crawl inside the covers and get me anyway. I could just picture Peter Hatcher telling the kids at school, *Did you hear about Sheila Tubman? She got bitten by a poisonous spider on her first night in Tarrytown. In twenty seconds she was dead!*

poisonous (poi•son•ous)—very harmful to life and health.

stop and organize

What 2 things have happened up to this point?

1.

2.

Response Notes

OTHERWISE KNOWN AS SHEILA THE GREAT (continued)

I jumped out of bed and ran down the hall to my parents' room. Daddy was snoring. I touched him on the shoulder. He sat right up in bed. "What? What is it?" he asked.

"It's just me, Daddy," I told him.

"Sheila . . . what do you want? It's the middle of the night."

"I can't sleep, Daddy. There's a spider on my ceiling."

Mom rolled over. She made a noise like *ummm.*

"Shush," Daddy said. "Go back to bed. I'll get it in the morning."

"But, Daddy, he could fall on me. Maybe he's poisonous."

"Oh . . . all right," Daddy said, kicking off the covers.

We walked down the hall together.

© GREAT SOURCE. COPYING IS PROHIBITED.

stop and organize

Who are 2 characters in the story? What have you learned about each one?

1.

2.

OTHERWISE KNOWN AS SHEILA THE GREAT (continued)

Response Notes

"How did you <u>notice</u> a spider on your ceiling in the middle of the night?" Daddy asked.

"I have my light on."

Daddy didn't ask me why.

When we got to my room he said, "Okay, where's your spider?"

At first I didn't see him. But then he started running across my ceiling.

notice (no•tice)—find or see.

"There he is!" I pointed. "You see?"

Daddy picked up one of my shoes.

"Hurry," I said.

Daddy stood on my bed, but when he smacked my shoe against the ceiling the spider ran the other way.

I tried to help. I gave him directions. "That's it," I called. "Now just a little to the left. No, no, now to the right. Hit him, Daddy! Hit him now!"

But Daddy missed him every time. He was running up and down my bed, but the spider ran faster.

Just as Daddy said, "I give up," he got him. Squish . . . that was the end of my spider. There was a big black mark on the ceiling. But I felt a whole lot better.

"Now, would you please go back to sleep!" Daddy said.

"I'll try."

"And if you find anything else unusual . . . tell me about it in the morning."

!!* stop and organize !*!*!*!*!*

What is Sheila's problem? How is it solved?

1.	2.

OTHERWISE KNOWN AS SHEILA THE GREAT (continued)

Response Notes

"Okay," I said, snuggling under the covers.

I think I fell asleep then. But a few hours later I woke up. I heard this really scary noise. It sounded like *whooo whooo whooo*. I didn't know what to do.

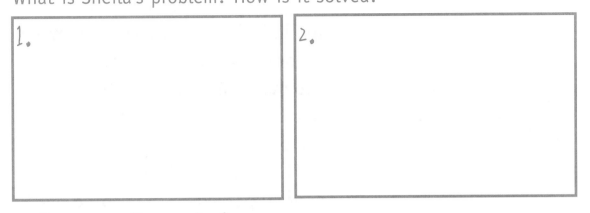

I buried my head under the pillow, but that didn't help. I could still hear it. I thought about what it might be—a ghost, or a vampire, or even an ordinary monster.

I got up and ran back down the hall. Daddy was snoring much louder now. This time I walked around to Mom's side of the bed and shook her a little. She jumped up.

"Oh, Sheila!" she said, when she saw who it was. "You scared me!"

"I'm sorry," I whispered.

"What is it?"

"It's a noise in my room," I said.

"Go back to sleep," Mom told me. "It's nothing."

"How do you know?" I asked. "You haven't heard it. It sounds like a ghost."

"There aren't any ghosts!"

"Please, Mom, please come and see."

"Oh . . . all right." She put on her robe and we went down the hall to my room. "Well," Mom said, "where's your noise?"

"Just wait," I told her.

She sat down on my bed and yawned. Soon it started again. *Whooo . . . whooo. . . .*

OTHERWISE KNOWN AS SHEILA THE GREAT (continued)

"You see?" I said, throwing my arms around Mom. I could tell from her face that she didn't like the noise either. "You want me to go wake Daddy?" I asked.

"No, not yet," Mom said. "First I'll have a look around myself. Hand me that baseball bat in the corner."

"For what?" I asked.

"Just in case," Mom said.

I gave Mom the bat. She held it like she was ready to use it. We waited until we heard the noise again. *Whooo . . . whooo . . . whooo. . . .*

"That's coming from outside," Mom said.

"So it's an outside ghost," I told her.

She went to the window. She stood there for a minute before she started to laugh.

!!* stop and organize !*!*!*!*

What 3 things happened after Sheila's dad killed the spider? Put the events in order in the storyboard boxes.

1.	2.	3.

Response Notes

OTHERWISE KNOWN AS SHEILA THE GREAT (continued)

"What's funny?" I asked.

"Oh, Sheila . . . just look!"

I hid behind her and peeked out the window. There was a beautiful silver moon. And there was also Jennifer, with her head held high. *She* was making those noises.

"What is she doing?" I asked. "Is she crazy?"

"She's baying at the moon," Mom said.

"What's baying?"

"It's like singing."

OTHERWISE KNOWN AS SHEILA THE
GREAT (continued)

"You mean she is going to stand there and make that ghost noise all summer?"

"I think so," Mom said.

"I told you to get rid of her, didn't I?" I said. "Who needs her? Who needs her making scary noises at me?"

"Come on, Sheila," Mom said, putting the baseball bat back in the corner. "Get into bed."

She tucked me in. I felt very tired.

"Now go to sleep."

"I'll try, " I said.

reread

Read *Otherwise Known As Sheila the Great* again. Be sure you understand what happened to Sheila and why she was scared. Be sure that you've answered the **Stop and Organize** questions.

WORD WORK

Many one-syllable words (words with 1 beat) are like the word *clip*. The word ends in one consonant letter, and a vowel comes right before the final consonant.

c l <u>i p</u>

When you add a suffix that starts with a vowel to words like *clip*, the base word changes. The last consonant is doubled, so the base word looks strange: *clipped*.

stop + ing = *stopping*

rot + ing = *rotting*

1. Add suffixes to the one-syllable words below.
2. Follow the rule and double that final consonant.

1. run + ing =
2. sit + ing =
3. bat + ed =
4. put + ing =
5. big + er =
6. rip + ed =

GET READY TO WRITE

A. LOOK AT A CHARACTER

A character trait tells you what a person is like—shy, brave, honest, mean.

1. Fill in the character map below.
2. Use clues from the story to tell about Sheila and what kind of a person she is.

HOW WAS SHE SCARED?

The spider and noises scare Sheila.

HOW WAS SHE IMAGINATIVE?

HOW WAS SHE A TROUBLEMAKER?

Sheila

WHY DIDN'T SHE GIVE UP?

B. PLAN

Get ready to write a narrative paragraph that tells about a time you were afraid. Fill in the details below.

Setting (Where? When?):

Problem:

Solution (How the problem was solved):

C. CREATE A TITLE

Now create a title for your narrative paragraph.

IV. WRITE

Write a **narrative paragraph** that tells about a time you were afraid.
1. Make sure you include details that make the setting, the problem, and the solution clear.
2. Use the Writers' Checklist to edit your paragraph.

Title:

Continue writing on the next page.

Continue your paragraph.

WRITERS' CHECKLIST

Apostrophes

☐ Did you use an apostrophe (') and an *s* to show possession or ownership of singular nouns? Examples: *The dog's tail was shaking. Tim's book fell to the floor.*

V. LOOK BACK

What made *Otherwise Known As Sheila the Great* easy or hard for you to read? Write your answer below.

Think about Your Reading

READERS' CHECKLIST

Ease

☐ Was the reading easy to read?

☐ Were you able to read it smoothly?

15

Hawk, I'm Your Brother

Have you ever dreamed of flying? How would the wind feel on your face? What would you see and hear? Take a flying trip with Rudy Soto and dream with him.

I. BEFORE YOU READ

Get ready to read by previewing.
1. First, read the title and the first 3 lines.
2. Then quickly look over the rest of the reading and study the pictures.
3. With your reading partner, talk about what Rudy Soto's dream of flying is like.

Why might Rudy want to fly?

_____

_____

_____

_____

_____

What are 2 reasons you would want to fly?

1. _____

_____

_____

2. _____

_____

_____

MY PURPOSE

What is Rudy Soto's dream of flying like? Why might he want to fly?

READ

Read "Hawk, I'm Your Brother."
1. Circle parts that describe what Rudy thinks flying would be like and why he'd like to try it.
2. Read the selection a second time. This time **connect** Rudy's dreams to your own feelings about what it would be like to fly. Jot comments in the Notes.

"Hawk, I'm Your Brother"
by Byrd Baylor

Rudy Soto
dreams
of flying . . .

wants
to <u>float</u>
on the wind,
wants
to <u>soar</u>
over <u>canyons</u>.

He doesn't see himself
some little
light-winged bird
that flaps
and <u>flutters</u>
when it flies.

float—hang weightless.
soar—fly high.
canyons (can•yons)—deep breaks in the surface of the earth, with steep, rocky walls.
flutters (flut•ters)—flies with a quick, light movement of the wings.

Response Notes

EXAMPLE:

I would like to fly in the wind like a kite.

171

"HAWK, I'M YOUR BROTHER" (continued)

No <u>cactus wren</u>.
No <u>sparrow</u>.

He'd be
more like
a HAWK

<u>gliding</u>

smoother
than anything else
in the world.

STOP AND RETELL stop and retell **STOP AND RETELL**

What does Rudy Soto dream of doing and being?

STOP AND RETELL STOP AND RETELL STOP AND RETELL STOP AND

He sees himself
a hawk
wrapped up in wind

lifting

cactus wren (cac•tus wren)—small, brown
    songbird.
sparrow (spar•row)—small brown or grey bird.
gliding (glid•ing)—flying smoothly.

"HAWK, I'M YOUR BROTHER" (continued)

facing the sun.

That's how
he wants
to fly.

That's all
he wants—
the only wish
he's ever had.

No matter what happens
he won't give it up.
He won't trade it
for easier wishes.

There,
playing alone
on the mountainside,
a dark skinny boy
calling out
to a hawk . . .

That's Rudy Soto.

What is so hard about Rudy Soto's only wish?

STOP AND RETELL STOP AND RETELL STOP AND RETELL

Response Notes

"HAWK, I'M YOUR BROTHER" (continued)

People here say
that the day he was born
he looked at the sky
and lifted his hands
toward birds
and seemed to smile
at Santos Mountain.

The first words
he ever learned
were the words for
FLYING
and for
BIRD
and for
UP THERE . . . UP THERE.

And later on
they say that
every day
he asked his father,
"When do I learn to fly?"

"HAWK, I'M YOUR BROTHER" (continued)

(He was too young then
to know
he'd never get his wish.)

His father said
"You run.
You climb over rocks.
You jump around like a crazy
<u>whirlwind</u>.
Why do you need to fly?"

"I just do.
I need to fly."

In those days
he thought that
somebody
would give him
the answer.
He asked
everybody . . .

everybody.

And they always said,
"People don't fly."

whirlwind (whirl•wind)—fast-moving and
destructive wind, like a tornado.

"HAWK, I'M YOUR BROTHER" (continued)

"Never?"

"Never."

But Rudy Soto
told them this:
"Some people do.
Maybe we just don't know
those people.
Maybe they live
far away from here."

And when he met new people
he would
look at them
carefully.

"Can you fly?"

They'd only laugh
and shake their heads.

Finally he learned
to stop
asking.

Still,
he thought
that maybe

flying
is the secret
old people
keep
to themselves.
Maybe they go sailing
quietly
through the sky
when children
are asleep.

Or maybe
flying
is for
magic people.

And he even thought
that if no one else
in the world
could fly
he'd be the one
who would learn it.

"Somebody ought to,"
he said.
"Somebody.
Me!
Rudy Soto."

There,
barefoot
on the mountainside
he'd
almost
fly.

He'd dream
he knew
the power
of great wings
and sing
up to the sun.

In his mind
he always seemed
to be a hawk,
the way he flew.

STOP AND RETELL **stop and retell** STOP AND RETELL

What are 3 things you have learned about Rudy Soto?

reread

Reread "Hawk, I'm Your Brother." Check to make sure you understand what Rudy thinks flying would be like and why he might like to fly. Be sure you have answered the **Stop and Retell** questions.

WORD WORK

There are many **contractions** in "Hawk, I'm Your Brother." Contractions are shortened forms of 2 words. The apostrophe (') takes the place of the missing letter(s).

he is = *he's*   could not = *couldn't*   I am = *I'm*

1. Read each pair of words in the chart below.
2. Write the contraction for these words. Hint: All of the contractions appear in "Hawk, I'm Your Brother."

Two Words	Contraction
that is	
will not	
he would	
they would	
do not	

© GREAT SOURCE. COPYING IS PROHIBITED.

READING REMINDER

Finding a way to relate to characters and events in stories can help you enjoy and remember what you read.

III. GET READY TO WRITE

BRAINSTORM

Get ready to write a paragraph about a flying adventure you might dream about.

1. Add at least 3 ideas to each box.

2. List 2 possible titles for your paragraph.

HOW CAN I FLY?

. in a balloon

. on a bird's back

. on a kite

WHERE WILL I GO?

HOW WILL FLYING FEEL? (flying) **WHAT WILL I SEE?**

Title Ideas:

1.

2.

WRITE

Write a **descriptive paragraph** about a flying adventure you might dream about.

1. Write a title and an opening sentence that tells how you will fly and where you will go.
2. Include ideas from your notes on page 180 and write a closing sentence that tells why you liked this adventure.
3. Use the Writers' Checklist to edit your paragraph.

Title:

Continue writing on the next page.

Continue your paragraph.

....

....

....

....

....

....

....

....

WRITERS' CHECKLIST

Apostrophes

☐ **Did you correctly form the possessive of plural words that do not end in *s*? Remember to add an apostrophe (') and an *s*.**
EXAMPLES: *mice's tails, women's voices*

V. LOOK BACK

What did you learn from this reading? Write your answer below.

....

....

....

....

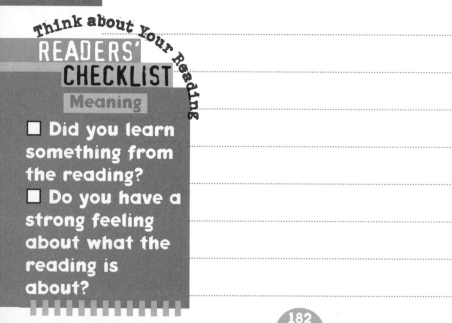

Think about Your Reading

READERS' CHECKLIST

Meaning

☐ **Did you learn something from the reading?**
☐ **Do you have a strong feeling about what the reading is about?**

....

....

....

....

16

Fun
and
By Myself

Reading and listening to poems can change your mood and your feelings. Watch what happens to your mood and feelings as you read the poems in this lesson.

Close your eyes and think about all the people, places, and things it might be fun to be. Use your imagination.

1. Talk to your reading partner and trade ideas.
2. Now fill in the headings of the web below. A few examples have been done for you.

THINGS I WANT TO BE

- a red convertible

PEOPLE I WANT TO BE

- an astronaut on the moon

What I'd Like to Be

PLACES I WANT TO BE

- at the top of a roller coaster

MY PURPOSE
What is each poem saying to me?

READ

Read the poems to yourself.

1. Next, take turns with your reading partner and read each poem out loud. Think about what each poem means to you and circle details you really like.

2. As you read each poem again, in the Notes, **draw** a picture of descriptions you enjoy.

"Fun" by Eloise Greenfield

The <u>pedal</u> on our school piano
    squeaks
And one day Miss Allen stopped
    playing
And we stopped singing
And Mr. Cobb came with the
    skinny, silver can
And gave it a long, greasy drink
And the next day when we got
    ready to sing

Response Notes

EXAMPLE:

pedal (ped•al)—bar pressed by the foot that changes the sound of a piano.

"FUN" (continued)

Miss Allen smiled
    and blinked her eyes
    and <u>plinked</u> the piano
    and pushed the pedal
And the pedal said
    SQUEEEEEEEAK!
And we laughed
But Miss Allen didn't

DOUBLE-ENTRY JOURNAL

Quote	What You Think This Means
"And we laughed / But Miss Allen didn't"	

Response Notes

"By Myself"
by Eloise Greenfield

When I'm by myself
And I close my eyes
I'm a twin
I'm a <u>dimple</u> in a chin
I'm a room full of toys
I'm a squeaky noise

plinked—played a few keys on.
dimple (dim•ple)—small
    hollow place in the skin or cheek.

"BY MYSELF" (continued)

I'm a <u>gospel song</u>
I'm a <u>gong</u>
I'm a leaf turning red
I'm a loaf of brown bread
I'm a whatever I want to be
An anything I care to be
And when I open my eyes
What I care to be
Is me

gospel song (gos•pel song)—religious
    song, sometimes sung in church.
gong—musical instrument that consists of a
    metal disk that is hit with a padded hammer.

DOUBLE-ENTRY JOURNAL

Quote	What You Think This Means
"What I care to be / Is me"	

reread

Read "Fun" and "By Myself" again. Think about what each
poem means to you. Be sure you have written down your
thoughts in the **Double-entry Journals**.

WORD WORK

If you can read one word, then you can read a word that's almost the same.

Example: You can read *hum*. Now take off the *h* and put *pl* in front of *um*. The new word is *plum*.

1. Make 3 new words for each word.
2. Change the beginning consonant letter or consonant cluster. One has been done for you.

chin	red
1. grin	1.
2.	2.
3.	3.

drink	sing
1.	1.
2.	2.
3.	3.

READING REMINDER

Reading or listening to a poem out loud and thinking about the pictures that come to mind can help you connect to a poem.

GET READY TO WRITE

A. BRAINSTORM IDEAS

Get ready to write a poem of your own using "By Myself" as a model.

1. Brainstorm a list of things you want to be. Use your web on page 184 for ideas.
2. Two examples have been done for you. Add more ideas of your own.

What I'd Like to Be

- a pounding drum to wake my brother's sleep
- the sour lemon juice squeezed over ice

B. CREATE A TITLE

Eloise Greenfield's poem is called "By Myself."
1. Think about what other titles might be interesting.
2. Write 2 possible titles for your poem below.

1.

2.

IV. WRITE

Write a draft of a **poem** on the page below.
1. Give your poem a title.
2. The first 2 lines have been written already.
3. After that, use some of the ideas you wrote about on page 189.
4. Use the Writers' Checklist to edit your poem.

Title:

When I'm by myself
And I close my eyes

Continue writing on the next page.

Continue writing your poem.

WRITERS' CHECKLIST

Apostrophes

☐ **Did you use apostrophes correctly in forming the possessive form of plural words that end in *s*? Remember to add only an apostrophe to words that already end in *s*.**
EXAMPLES: *the leaves' sharp edges, the cats' skinny tails*

V. LOOK BACK

What would you tell a friend about these poems? Write your answer below.

READERS' CHECKLIST

Understanding

■ **Did you understand the readings?**
■ **Can you tell a friend what the readings are about?**

Acknowledgments

6, 7, 8, 9 "Little Pine," "Goose," "Spring Sleep," "Moon," from MIST (c) 1996 by Minfong Ho. Used by permission of HarperCollins Publishers.

13 *Booker T. Washington,* from BOOKER T. WASHINGTON by Patricia and Fredrick McKissack. Copyright © 1992 by Patricia and Fredrick McKissack. Reprinted by permission of Enslow Publishers.

23 *Gloria's Way,* from "The Question," from GLORIA'S WAY by Ann Cameron. Copyright © 2000 by Ann Cameron. Reprinted by permission of Farrar, Straus and Giroux, LLC.

35 *Train to Somewhere,* from TRAIN TO SOMEWHERE by Eve Bunting. Text copyright © 1986 by Eve Bunting. Reprinted by permission of Clarion Books/Houghton Mifflin Company. All rights reserved.

49 *First Flight,* text copyright © 1997 by George Shea. Illustrations copyright © 1997 by Dan Bolognese. Used by permission of HarperCollins Publishers.

59 *A Drop of Blood,* text copyright © 1967 by Paul Showers. Used by permission of HarperCollins Publishers.

69 *A River Dream,* from A RIVER DREAM. Copyright © 1988 by Allen Say. Reprinted by permission of Houghton Mifflin Company. All rights reserved.

79 *How We Learned the Earth Is Round* From HOW WE LEARNED THE EARTH IS ROUND by Patricia Lauber. Copyright © 1990 by Patricia Lauber. Used by permission of HarperCollins Publishers.

89 *I Am Rosa Parks,* from ROSA PARKS: MY STORY by Rosa Parks with Jim Haskins. Copyright © 1992 by Rosa Parks. Used by permission of Dial Books for Young Readers, a division of Penguin Putnam Inc.

99 *Germs Make Me Sick!,* text copyright © 1985, 1995 by Melvin Berger. Used by permission of HarperCollins Publishers.

109 *The Skirt,* from THE SKIRT by Gary Soto. Copyright © 1992 by Gary Soto. Used by permission of Random House Children's Books, a division of Random House, Inc.

121 *Through Grandpa's Eyes,* text copyright © 1980 by Patricia MacLachlan. Used by permission of HarperCollins Publishers.

133 *Me and My Shadow,* from Me and My Shadow by Arthur Dorros. Copyright © 1990 by Arthur Dorros. Reprinted by permission of Scholastic Inc.

143 *Follow That Trash!,* from FOLLOW THAT TRASH! by Francine Jacobs, illustrated by Mavis Smith. Copyright © 1996 by Francine Jacobs. Used by permission of Grosset & Dunlap, Inc., a division of Penguin Putnam Inc.

153 *Otherwise Known As Sheila the Great,* from OTHERWISE KNOWN AS SHEILA THE GREAT by Judy Blume. Copyright © 1972 by Judy Blume. Used by permission of Dutton Children's Books, a division of Penguin Putnam Inc.

171 "Hawk, I'm Your Brother," from HAWK, I'M YOUR BROTHER by Byrd Baylor. Reprinted with the permission of Atheneum Books for Young Readers, an imprint of Simon & Schuster Publishing Division. Text copyright © 1996 by Byrd Baylor.

185, 186 "Fun" and "By Myself" from HONEY, I LOVE by Eloise Greenfield. Text copyright © 1978 by Eloise Greenfield. Illustrations copyright © 1978 by Dianne and Leo Dillon. Used by permission of HarperCollins Publishers. "Fun" by Eloise Greenfield. Text copyright © 1978 by Eloise Greenfield. Illustrations copyright © 1978 by Dianne and Leo Dillon. Used by permission of HarperCollins Publishers.

Cover Photography:
All photos © Eileen Ryan.

Illustration:
Chapter One: Ralph Canaday
Chapter Two: Donna Catanesse
Chapter Five: Victor Kennedy
Chapter Seven: Brad Teare
Chapter Eight: Reggie Holladay
Chapter Nine: Mike Dammer
Chapter Ten: Morella Fuenmayor
Chapter Eleven: Judy Stead
Chapter Twelve: George Hamblin
Chapter Thirteen: Tom McKee
Chapter Fourteen: Ilene Richard
Chapter Sixteen: Patti Green

Cover and Book Design:
Christine Ronan, Sean O'Neill, and Maria Mariottini, Ronan Design

Permissions:
Feldman and Associates

Developed by Nieman Inc.

Author/Title **Index**

The editors have made every effort to trace the ownership of all copyrighted selections found in this book and to make full acknowledgment for their use. Omissions brought to our attention will be corrected in a subsequent edition